The
Lip Reading Thesaurus
of
3000
Look-alike Words

compiled by Tony Edens

Also in this series:
- Lip Reading a self-help textbook
- The Lip Reading Dictionary
- Word Puzzles for lip reading students
- The Lip Readers' Picture Book of
  mis-heard phrases

NOTES

The thesaurus entries are in three columns containing:

1. Entries in alphabetical order.
2. Sequences of lip shapes.
3. List of words that look identical or similar to the lip reader.

Words in **Roman** type look **identical** on the lips.

Words in *Italic* type look **similar** on the lips.

Words in **CAPITALS** are **names** of people or places.

This book is based on a dictionary of about ten thousand commonly used words of which over three thousand are found to have identical or very similar lip shapes. So based on this sample we can say that about 30% of spoken language is abiguous to the lip reader.

Shaping and movement of the lips in conversation is dictated by sounds used in speech and these in turn are variable according to regional accents. Users should exercise caution when selecting look-alike samples for lip reading teaching or practice and check that the lip shapes and sounds, particularly of the vowels, match what is commonly used in the place they live.

a bait	*u. m.ay.t.*	a bait, *abate*
a ball	*u. m.aw.l.*	a ball, able
a board	*u. m.aw.t.*	a board, a port, aboard
a bound	*u. m.ow.t.t.*	a bound, a mount, *abound, amount*
a gate	*u. k.ay.t.*	a gate, again
a mount	*u. m.ow.t.t.*	abound, amount, *abound, amount*
a port	*u. m.aw.t.*	a board, a port, aboard
a.m.	*ay.e.m.*	a.m., *aim*
abbey	*a.m.ee.*	abbey, happy, gammy
able	*ay.m.l.*	able, *a ball, cable, gable*
aboard	*u.m.aw.t.*	a board, a port, aboard
abode	*a.m.oh.t.*	abode, a boat, a bone
abound	*u.m.ow.t.t.*	abound, amount, *a bound, a mount*
abreast	*a.m.r.e.s.t.*	abreast, *oppressed*
absent	*a.m.s.e.t.t.*	absend, absent,
abuse	*a.m.y.oo.s.*	abuse, amuse
abused	*a.m.ew.s.t.*	abused, amused
abyss	*a.m.i.s.*	abyss, amiss
accent	*a.s.s.e.t.t.*	accent, *ascend, ascent, assent*
accept	*a.s.e.m.t.*	accept, *exempt*
accepted	*a.s.e.m.t.e.t.*	accepted, *exempted*

access

access	*a.s.e.s.*	access, *asses, axes*
ache	*ay.k.*	ache, age
aching	*ay.k.i.ng.*	aching, aging
acted	*a.k.t.i.t.*	acted, *artic', attic*
acts	*a.k.t.s.*	acts, *axe*
acute	*a.k.ew.t.*	acute, argued
add	*a.t.*	add, an, and, art, at, aunt, *card, cart, guard, hard, heart*
addle	*a.t.l.*	addle, *angle, ankle*
address	*a.t.r.e.s.*	address, *undress*
addressed	*a.t.r.e.s.t.*	addressed, *undressed*
addressing	*a.t.r.e.s.i.ng.*	addressing, *undressing*
adds	*a.t.s.*	adds, arts
admire	*a.t.m.ii.r.*	admire, *empire*
advice	*a.t.v.ii.s.*	advice, advise
advise	*a.t.v.ii.s.*	advice, advise
again	*u.k.ay.t.*	a gate, again
age	*ay.j.*	ache, age
aged	*ay.j.t.*	ached, aged
aid	*ay.t.*	aid, ate, eight, *gate, hate, Kate*
aids	*ay.t.s.*	aids, *gates, hates, Kate's*
aim	*ay.m.*	aim ape

aim	*ay.m.*	aim, *a.m.*
aiming	*ay.m.i.ng.*	aiming, aping
air	*air.*	air, heir
alder	*aw.l.t.er.*	alder, altar, alter
alight	*a.l.ii.t.*	alight, allied
allied	*a.l.ii.t.*	alight, allied
altar	*aw.l.t.er.*	alder, altar, alter
alter	*aw.l.t.er.*	alder, altar, alter
amber	*a.m.m.er.*	amber, camber, camper
ambles	*a.m.m.uu.l.s.*	ambles, apples
amiss	*a.m.i.s.*	abyss, amiss
amount	*u.m.ow.t.t.*	abound, amount, *a bound, a mount*
ample	*a.m.m.l.*	amble, ample
amuse	*u.m.ew.s.*	abuse, amuse
amused	*a.m.ew.s.t.*	abused, amused
an	*a.t.*	add, an, and, art, at, aunt, *card, cart, guard, hard, heart*
anchor	*a.t.k.er.*	anchor, *anger*
anchors	*a.ng.k.er.s.*	anchors, *angers*
ancient	*ay.t.j.u.t.t.*	ancient, *engine*

and

and	*a.t.t.*	add, an, and, art, at, aunt, *card, cart, guard, hard, heart*
and	*a.t.t.*	and, ant, aunt, *can't*
anger	*a.ng.k.er.*	anchor, anger
angers	*a.ng.k.er.s.*	anchors, angers
angle	*a.ng.k.l.*	angle, ankle
angles	*a.ng.k.uu.l.s.*	angles, ankles
ankle	*a.ng.k.l.*	angle, ankle
ankles	*a.ng.k.l.s.*	angles, ankles
any	*e.t.ee.*	any, *eddy*
appealing	*a.m.ia.l.i.ng.*	appealing, annealing
apple	*a.m.l.*	apple, amble, ample
apples	*a.m.l.s.*	apples, ambles
applied	*a.m.l.ii.t.*	applied, *applies*
applies	*a.m.l.ii.s.*	applies, *applied*
approach	*a.m.r.oh.j.*	approach, a broach
arctic	*a.k.t.i.k.*	acted, artic', attic
argued	*a.k.ew.t.*	acute, argued
arm	*a.m.*	arm, *harp*
armed	*a.m.t.*	armed, *harped*
arms	*a.m.s.*	arms, *harps*
arrival	*a.r.ii.v.l.*	arrival, a rifle

art	*a.t.*	add, an, and, art, at, aunt, *card, cart, guard, hard, heart*
arts	*a.t.s.*	adds, arts, aunts
as	*a.s.*	as, ass, axe, *add, an, and, at*
ascend	*a.s.e.t.t.*	accent, ascend, ascent, assent
ascended	*a.s.e.t.t.e.t.*	ascended, assented
ascent	*a.s.e.t.t.*	accent, ascend, ascent, assent
aside	*a.s.ii.t.*	aside, a sign, a sight
ass	*a.s.*	as, ass, axe, *add, an, and, at*
assent	*a.s.e.t.t.*	accent, ascend, ascent, assent
assented	*a.s.e.t.t.i.t.*	ascended, assented
asses	*a.s.e.s.*	access, asses, axes
at	*a.t.*	add, an, and, art, at, aunt, *card, cart, guard, hard, heart*
ate	*ay.t.*	aid, ate, eight, *gate, hate, Kate*
attendance	*a.t.e.t.t.a.t.s.*	attendance, attandants
attendants	*a.t.e.t.t.a.t.t.s.*	attendance, attandants
attic	*a.t.i.k.*	acted, artic, attic
aught	*aw.t.*	aught, awed, awn, ought

aunt

aunt	*a.t.t.*	add, an, and, art, at, aunt, *card, cart, guard, hard, heart*
aunt	*a.t.t.*	and, ant, aunt, can't
awe	*aw.*	awe, oar, or
awed	*aw.t.*	aught, awed, awn, ought
awn	*aw.t.*	aught, awed, awn, ought
axe	*a.s.*	acts, *axe*
axe	*a.s.*	as, ass, axe, *add, an, and, at*
axes	*a.s.i.s.*	access, asses, axes
baby	*m.ay.m.ee.*	baby, maybe
back	*m.a.k.*	back, bag, mark, pack, park
backed	*m.a.k.t.*	backed, bagged, barked, marked, packed, parked
backer	*m.a.k.er.*	backer, barker, marker, packer, parker
backing	*m.a.k.i.ng.*	backing, packing
backs	*m.a.k.s.*	backs, bags, barks, marks, parks
bacon	*m.ay.k.u.t.*	bacon, *taken*
bad	*m.a.t.*	bad, ban, bard, barn, bat, mad, man, mat, pad, pan, part, pat

badder	*m.a.t.er.*	badder, banner, barter, batter, madder, manner, manor, matter, padder, patter
bade	*m.ay.t.*	bade, bait, bane, made, maid, main, mane, mate, paid, pain, pane
badge	*m.a.j.*	badge, barge, batch, march, marsh, mash, match, patch
badger	*m.a.j.er.*	badger, masher
badges	*m.a.j.i.s.*	badges, barges, maches, marches, marshes, patches
badly	*m.a.t.l.ee.*	badly, manly, partly
bag	*m.a.k.*	back, bag, mark, pack, park
bagged	*m.a.k.t.*	backed, bagged, barked, marked, packed, parked
bags	*m.a.k.s.*	backs, bags, barks, marks, parks
bail	*m.ay.l.*	bail, mail, male, pail, pale
bails	*m.ay.l.s.*	bails, mails, males, pails
bait	*m.ay.t.*	bade, bait, bane, made, maid, main, mane, mate, paid, pain, pane
baits	*m.ay.t.s.*	baits, banes, maids, mains, manes, mates, pains

bake

bake	*m.ay.k.*	bake, make
baker	*m.ay.k.er.*	baker, maker
bakers	*m.ay.k.er.s.*	bakers, makers
bakes	*m.ay.k.s.*	bakes, makes
baking	*m.ay.k.i.ng.*	baking, making
bald	*m.aw.l.t.*	bald, malt, mauled
balding	*m.aw.l.t.i.ng.*	balding, *bolting, moulding*
ball	*m.aw.l.*	ball, mall, pall
balm	*m.a.m.*	balm, *map,* palm
balmed	*m.a.m.t.*	balmed, barbed, mapped, palmed
balms	*m.a.m.s.*	balms, barbs, maps, palms
ban	*m.a.t.*	bad, ban, bard, barn, bat, mad, man, mat, pad, pan, part, pat
band	*m.a.t.t.*	band, banned, manned, panned, pant, part
bane	*m.ay.t.*	bade, bait, bane, made, maid, main, mane, mate, paid, pain, pane
banes	*m.ay.t.s.*	baits, banes, maids, mains, manes, mates, pains
banned	*m.a.t.t.*	band, banned, manned, panned, pant, part

banner	*m.a.t.er.*	badder, banner, barter, batter, madder, manner, manor, matter, padder, pander, patter
banners	*m.a.t.er.s.*	banners, manners, matters, panders, patters
bannish	*m.a.t.i.j.*	bannish, *marriage,parish*
banns	*m.a.t.s.*	banns, barns, man's, pads, pans, pants, parts
bantered	*m.a.t.t.er.t.*	bantered, battered, mattered, pattern, patterned
barbed	*m.a.m.t.*	balmed, barbed, mapped, palmed
barbs	*m.a.m.s.*	balms, barbs, maps, palms
bard	*m.a.t.*	bad, ban, bard, barn, bat, mad, man, mat, pad, pan, part, pat
bare	*m.air.*	bare, bear, mare, pair, pare, pear
barge	*m.a.j.*	badge, barge, batch, march, marsh, mash, match, patch
barges	*m.a.j.e.s.*	badges, barges, matches, marches, marshes, patches
baring	*m.air.i.ng.*	baring, bearing, paring

barked

barked	*m.a.k.t.*	backed, bagged, barked, marked, packed, parked
barker	*m.a.k.er.*	backer, barker, marker, packer, parker
barks	*m.a.k.s.*	backs, bags, barks, marks, parks
barn	*m.a.t.*	bad, ban, bard, barn, bat, mad, man, mat, pad, pan, part, pat
barns	*m.a.t.s.*	banns, barns, man's, pads, pans, pants, parts
barred	*m.a.r.t.*	barred, marred
barrow	*m.a.r.oh.*	barrow, marrow
barrows	*m.a.r.oh.s.*	barrows, marrows
bars	*m.a.s.*	bars, pass, *marks*
barter	*m.a.t.er.*	badder, banner, barter, batter, madder, manner, manor, matter, padder, patter
base	*m.ay.s.*	base, bass, mace, pace, pays
based	*m.ay.s.t.*	based, paste
bases	*m.ay.s.i.s.*	bases, basis, mazes, paces
basis	*m.ay.s.i.s.*	bases, basis, mazes, paces
bass	*m.ay.s.*	base, bass, mace, pace, pays

bat	*m.a.t.*	bad, ban, bard, barn, bat, mad, man, mat, pad, pan, part, pat
batch	*m.a.j.*	badge, barge, batch, march, marsh, mash, match, patch
bath	*m.a.th.*	bath, path
batted	*m.a.t.i.t.*	batted, matted, parted, patted
batter	*m.a.t.er.*	badder, banner, barter, batter, madder, manner, manor, matter, padder, patter
battered	*m.a.t.er.t.*	bantered, battered, mattered, pattern, patterned
battle	*m.a.t.l.*	battle, mantel, mantle, paddle, panel
bay	*m.ay.*	bay, may, pay
baying	*m.ay.i.ng.*	baying, paying
be	*m.ee.*	be, bee, me, pea
beach	*m.ee.j.*	beach, peach
beader	*m.ee.t.er.*	beader, beater, meter, metre, PETER
beads	*m.ee.t.s.*	beads, beans, beats, beets, means, meats, meets, peats
beamed	*m.ee.m.t.*	beamed, peeped

bean

bean	*m.ee.t.*	bean, beat, been, beet, mean, meat, meet, peat
beans	*m.ee.t.s.*	beads, beans, beats, beets, means, meats, meets, peats
bear	*m.air.*	bare, bear, mare, pair, pare, pear
bearing	*m.air.i.ng.*	baring, bearing, paring
beast	*m.ee.s.t.*	beast, pieced
beat	*m.ee.t.*	bean, beat, been, beet, mean, meat, meet, peat
beater	*m.ee.t.er.*	beader, beater, meter, metre, PETER
beating	*m.ee.t.i.ng.*	beating, meaning, meeting
beats	*m.ee.t.s.*	beads, beans, beats, beets, means, meats, meets, peats
beck	*m.e.k.*	beck, beg, peck, peg
bed	*m.e.t.*	bed, bet, men, met, pen, pet
beds	*m.e.t.s.*	beds, bets, men's, pence, pens, pets
bee	*m.ee.*	be, bee, me, pea
been	*m.ee.t.*	bean, beat, been, beet, mean, meat, meet, peat
beer	*m.ear.*	beer, bier, mere, peer, pier

bees	*m.ee.s.*	bees, peace, peas, piece
beet	*m.ee.t.*	bean, beat, been, beet, mean, meat, meet, peat
beets	*m.ee.t.s.*	beads, beans, beats, beets, means, meats, meets, peats
beg	*m.e.k.*	beck, beg, peck, peg
begging	*m.e.k.i.ng.*	begging, pegging, pecking
beige	*m.ay.j.*	beige, page
belief	*m.e.l.ee.v.*	belief, believe
believe	*m.e.l.ee.v.*	belief, believe
belt	*m.e.l.t.*	belt, melt, pelt
bend	*m.e.t.t.*	bend, bent, bet, men, meant, mend, met, pen, penned, pent, pet
bent	*m.e.t.t.*	bend, bent, bet, men, meant, mend, met, pen, penned, pent, pet
berry	*m.e.r.ee.*	berry, merry, perry
BERT	*M.ER.T.*	bird, BERT, burn, pert
best	*m.e.s.t.*	best, messed, pest
bet	*m.e.t.*	bed, bet, men, met, pen, pet
bet	*m.e.t.*	bend, bent, bet, men, meant, mend, met, pen, penned, pent, pet

bets

bets	*m.e.t.s.*	beds, bets, men's, pence, pens, pets
bib	*m.i.m.*	bib, pip
bibs	*m.i.m.s.*	bibs, pips
bid	*m.i.t.*	bid, bin, bit, mid, pin, pit
bide	*m.ii.t.*	bide, bind, bite, might, mind, mine, mite, pied
bids	*m.i.t.s.*	bids, bins, bits, mince, pins, pits
bier	*m.ee.er.*	beer, bier, mere, peer, pier
big	*m.i.k.*	big, MICK, pick, pig
bike	*m.ii.k.*	bike, MIKE, pike
bile	*m.ii.l.*	bile, mile, pile
biles	*m.ii.l.s.*	biles, miles, piles
bill	*m.i.l.*	bill, mill, pill
billed	*m.i.l.t.*	billed, build, built, milled, milt
billion	*m.i.l.ee.u.t.*	billion, million, pillion
billions	*m.i.l.ee.u.t.s.*	billions, millions
bills	*m.i.l.s.*	bills, mills, pills
bin	*m.i.t.*	bid, bin, bit, mid, pin, pit
bind	*m.ii.t.t.*	bide, bind, bite, might, mind, mine, mite, pied
binding	*m.ii.t.t.i.ng.*	binding, biting, mining,minding

binds	*m.ii.t.t.s.*	binds, bites, minds, mites, pints
bins	*m.i.t.s.*	bids, bins, bits, mince, pins, pits
birch	*m.er.j.*	birch, merge, perch
bird	*m.er.t.*	bird, BERT, burn, pert
birth	*m.er.th.*	birth, mirth, PERTH
bit	*m.i.t.*	bid, bin, bit, mid, pin, pit
bitch	*m.i.j.*	bitch, pitch
bite	*m.ii.t.*	bide, bind, bite, might, mind, mine, mite, pied, pined, pint
bites	*m.ii.t.s.*	binds, bites, minds, mites, pints
biting	*m.ii.t.i.ng.*	binding, biting, mining,minding
bits	*m.i.t.s.*	bids, bins, bits, mince, pins, pits
blade	*m.l.ay.t.*	blade, plain, plane, plate, played
blades	*m.l.ay.t.s.*	blades, plains, plates
blank	*m.l.a.ng.k.*	blank, plank
blaze	*m.l.ay.s.*	blaze, place, plays
blazing	*m.l.ay.s.i.ng.*	blazing, placing
bleated	*m.l.ee.t.i.t.*	bleated, pleaded, pleated

bleating

bleating	*m.l.ee.t.i.ng.*	bleeding, bleating, pleading, pleating
bleeding	*m.l.ee.t.i.ng.*	bleeding, bleating, pleading, pleating
blew	*m.l.oo.*	blew, blue
blight	*m.l.ii.t.*	blight, plight
blighted	*m.l.ii.t.i.t.*	blighted, plighted
bloat	*m.l.oh.t.*	bloat, blown
bloom	*m.l.oo.m.*	bloom, plume
blot	*m.l.o.t.*	blot, pled, plot
blots	*m.l.o.t.s.*	blots, plods, plots
blotters	*m.l.o.t.er.s.*	blotters, plodders, plotters
blotting	*m.l.o.t.i.ng.*	blotting, plodding, plotting
blown	*m.l.oh.t.*	bloat, blown
blub	*m.l.u.m.*	blub, plum
blubber	*m.l.u.m.er.*	blubber, plumber
blue	*m.l.oo.*	blew, blue
blunder	*m.l.u.t.t.er.*	blunder, blunter, plunder
blundered	*m.l.u.t.t.er.t.*	blundered, plundered
blundering	*m.l.u.t.t.er.i.ng.*	blundering, plundering
blunter	*m.l.u.t.t.er.*	blunder, blunter, plunder

board	*m.aw.t.*	board, bored, born, bourne, bought, moored, pawned, poured, port
boarded	*m.aw.t.e.t.*	boarded, ported
boarder	*m.aw.t.er.*	boarder, border, mortar, mourner, pawner, porter
boarding	*m.aw.t.i.ng.*	boarding, morning, mourning, pawning
boards	*m.aw.t.s.*	boards, ports
boast	*m.oh.s.t.*	boast, most, post
boasted	*m.oh.s.t.i.t.*	boasted, posted
boasting	*m.oh.s.t.i.ng.*	boasting, posting
boasts	*m.oh.s.t.s.*	boasts, posts
boat	*m.oh.t.*	boat, bode, bone, moan, moat, mode, mowed
boat	*m.oh.t.*	boat, bone, moan
boater	*m.oh.t.er.*	boater, motor
boaters	*m.oh.t.er.s.*	boaters, motors
boating	*m.oh.t.i.ng.*	boating, moaning
boats	*m.oh.t.s.*	boats, bones, moans
bob	*m.o.m.*	bob, bomb, mob, mop, pop, *pomp*
bobbing	*m.o.m.i.ng.*	bobbing, bombing, mobbing, mopping, popping

bode

bode	*m.oh.t.*	boat, bode, bone, moan, moat, mode, mowed
bold	*m.oh.l.t.*	bold, bolt, mould, moult, poult
bolt	*m.oh.l.t.*	bold, bolt, mould, moult, poult
bolted	*m.oh.l.t.i.t.*	bolted, moulded
bolting	*m.oh.l.t.i.ng.*	bolting, moulding, balding
bomb	*m.o.m.*	bob, bomb, mob, mop, pop, *pomp*
bombing	*m.o.m.i.ng.*	bobbing, bombing, mobbing, mopping, popping
bond	*m.o.t.t.*	bond, pond, *pot*
bone	*m.oh.t.*	boat, bode, bone, moan, moat, mode, mowed
bone	*m.oh.t.*	boat, bone, moan
boned	*m.oh.t.t.*	boned, moaned
bones	*m.oh.t.s.*	boats, bones, moans
bonnet	*m.o.t.e.t.*	bonnet, podded, potted
bony	*m.oh.t.ee.*	bony, pony
booed	*m.oo.t.*	booed, boon, boot, mood, moon, moot
boon	*m.oo.t.*	booed, boon, boot, mood, moon, moot

boon	*m.oo.t.*	boon, boot, mood, moon, moot
boons	*m.oo.t.s.*	boons, boots, moods, moons, moots
boot	*m.oo.t.*	booed, boon, boot, mood, moon, moot
boot	*m.oo.t.*	boon, boot, mood, moon, moot
booted	*m.oo.t.e.t.*	booted, mooted
boots	*m.oo.t.s.*	boons, boots, moods, moons, moots
border	*m.aw.t.er.*	boarder, border, mortar, mourner, pawner, porter
bore	*m.aw.*	bore, moor, more, poor, pore
bored	*m.aw.t.*	board, bored, born, bourne, bought, moored, pawned, poured, port
borer	*m.ow.r.er.*	borer, poorer
boring	*m.aw.r.i.ng.*	boring, mooring, pouring
born	*m.aw.t.*	board, bored, born, bourne, bought, moored, pawned, poured, port
borne	*m.aw.t.*	board, bored, born, bourne, bought, moored, pawned, poured, port
borrow	*m.o.r.oh.*	borrow, morrow
boss	*m.o.s.*	boss, box, moss, pox

bossed

bossed	*m.o.s.t.*	bossed, boxed, mossed, poxed
bosses	*m.o.s.i.s.*	bosses, boxes, mosses, poxes
bot	*m.o.t.*	bot, pod, pot, *pond*
bottle	*m.o.t.l.*	bottle, model, mottle
bottles	*m.o.t.l.s.*	bottles, models, mottles
bought	*m.aw.t.*	board, bored, born, bourne, bought, moored, pawned, poured, port
bounce	*m.ow.t.s.*	bounce, pounce, pouts, *bounds, pounds*
bound	*m.ow.t.t.*	bound, mound, mount, pound
bounds	*m.ow.t.t.s.*	bounds, mounts, pounds, *bounce, pounce*
bounds	*m.ow.t.t.s.*	bounds, pounds, *bounce, pounce, pouts,*
bower	*m.ow.er.*	bower, power
bowers	*m.ow.er.s.*	bowers, powers
bowl	*m.oh.l.*	bowl, mole, pole
bowls	*m.oh.l.s.*	bowls, moles, poles
bows	*m.oh.s.*	bows, pose
box	*m.o.s.*	boss, box, moss, pox
boxed	*m.o.s.t.*	bossed, boxed, mossed, poxed

boxes	m.o.s.e.s.	bosses, boxes, mosses, poxes
boys	m.oi.s.	boys, buoys, poise
brace	m.r.ay.s.	brace, braise, praise, prays
braces	m.r.ay.s.e.s.	braces, praises
braise	m.r.ay.s.	brace, braise, praise, prays
braising	m.r.ay.s.i.ng.	braising, praising
brake	m.r.ay.k.	brake, break
branch	m.r.a.t.j.	branch, *brash*
brash	m.r.a.j.	brash, *branch*
brawn	m.r.aw.t.	broad, brawn, brought, prawn
bray	m.r.ay.	bray, pray, prey
brayed	m.r.ay.t.	brayed, prayed, preyed
brazed	m.r.ay.s.t.	brazed, praised
break	m.r.ay.k.	brake, break
breast	m.r.e.s.t.	breast, pressed
brewed	m.r.oo.t.	brewed, brood, brute, prude, prune
brick	m.r.i.k.	brick, brig, prick, prig
bride	m.r.ii.t.	bride, bright, brine, pride
brig	m.r.i.k.	brick, brig, prick, prig
bright	m.r.ii.t.	bride, bright, brine, pride

brim

brim	*m.r.i.m.*	brim, prim
brine	*m.r.ii.t.*	bride, bright, brine, pride
broad	*m.r.aw.t.*	broad, brawn, brought, prawn
brood	*m.r.oo.t.*	brewed, brood, brute, prude, prune
brood	*m.r.oo.t.*	brood, brute, prude
brought	*m.r.aw.t.*	broad, brawn, brought, prawn
brow	*m.r.ow.*	brow, prow
browed	*m.r.ow.t.*	browed, brown, proud
brown	*m.r.ow.t.*	browed, brown, proud
brows	*m.r.ow.s.*	brows, browse, prows
browse	*m.r.ow.s.*	brows, browse, prows
brute	*m.r.oo.t.*	brewed, brood, brute, prude, prune
brute	*m.r.oo.t.*	brood, brute, prude
buck	*m.u.k.*	buck, bug, muck, mug, pug
bud	*m.u.t.*	bud, bun, but, butt, mud, pun, putt
bud	*m.u.t.*	bud, bun, but, butt, mud, pun, putt
budding	*m.u.t.i.ng.*	budding, bunting, butting, punning, punting, putting

budge	*m.u.j.*	budge, mush, much
buds	*m.u.t.s.*	buds, buns, butts, puns, putts
buffed	*m.u.v.t.*	buffed, muffed, puffed
buffer	*m.u.v.er.*	buffer, puffer
bug	*m.u.k.*	buck, bug, muck, mug, pug
build	*m.i.l.t.*	billed, build, built, milled, milt
built	*m.i.l.t.*	billed, build, built, milled, milt
bull	*m.uu.l.*	bull, pull
bulls	*m.uu.l.s.*	bulls, pulls
bully	*m.uu.l.ee.*	bully, pulley
bum	*m.u.m.*	bum, mum, pub, pup, *bump, pump*
bump	*m.u.m.m.*	bump, pump, *bum, mum, pub, pup*
bumped	*m.u.m.m.t.*	bumped, pumped
bumps	*m.u.m.m.s.*	bumps, mumps, pumps, *bums, mums, pubs, pups*
bun	*m.u.t.*	bud, bun, but, butt, mud, pun, putt
bun	*m.u.t.*	bud, bun, but, butt, mud, pun, putt
bunch	*m.u.t.j.*	bunch, munch, punch

bunny

bunny	*m.u.t.ee.*	bunny, money, muddy, putty
buns	*m.u.t.s.*	buds, buns, butts, puns, putts
bunting	*m.u.t.t.i.ng.*	budding, bunting, butting, punning, punting, putting
buoys	*m.oi.s.*	boys, buoys, poise
burden	*m.er.t.t.*	burden, burned, burnt
buried	*m.e.r.i.t.*	buried, merit
burn	*m.er.t.*	bird, BERT, burn, pert
burned	*m.er.t.t.*	burden, burned, burnt
burnt	*m.er.t.t.*	burden, burned, burnt
bursar	*m.er.s.er.*	bursar, purser
burst	*m.er.s.t.*	burst, person
bus	*m.u.s.*	bus, puss
bush	*m.uu.j.*	bush, push
bushed	*m.uu.j.t.*	bushed, pushed
bushes	*m.uu.j.i.s.*	bushes, pushes
bushing	*m.uu.j.i.ng.*	bushing, pushing
bushy	*m.uu.j.ee.*	bushy, pushy
bussed	*m.u.s.t.*	bussed, bust, must
bust	*m.u.st*	bussed, bust, must
bustle	*m.u.s.l.*	bustle, muscle, muzzle,

		puzzle
bustled	*m.u.s.uu.l.t.*	bustled, muscled, muzzled, puzzled
bustles	*m.u.s.uu.l.s.*	bustles, muscles, muzzles, puzzles
but	*m.u.t.*	bud, bun, but, butt, mud, pun, putt
but	*m.u.t.*	bud, bun, but, butt, mud, pun, putt
butt	*m.u.t.*	bud, bun, but, butt, mud, pun, putt
butt	*m.u.t.*	bud, bun, but, butt, mud, pun, putt
butter	*m.u.t.er.*	butter, mutter, putter
buttered	*m.u.t.er.t.*	buttered, muttered
butting	*m.u.t.i.ng.*	budding, bunting, butting, punning, punting, putting
button	*m.u.t.t.*	button, mutton
button	*m.u.t.t.*	button, mutton
butts	*m.u.t.s.*	buds, buns, butts, puns, putts
butts	*m.u.t.s.*	butts, putts
buy	*m.ii.*	buy, by, bye, my, pie
by	*m.ii.*	buy, by, bye, my, pie
bye	*m.ii.*	buy, by, bye, my, pie

cab

cab	*k.a.m.*	cab, calm, cam, cap, carp, gap, ham, harm, harp
cabin	*k.a.m.i.t.*	cabin, habit
cadge	*k.a.j.*	cadge, cash, hash, hatch
cake	*k.ay.k.*	cake, hake
calf	*k.a.v.*	calf, half, have
call	*k.aw.l.*	call, hall
called	*k.aw.l.t.*	called, halt, hauled, *calls*
calling	*k.aw.l.i.ng.*	calling, hauling
calls	*k.aw.l.s.*	calls, *called, halt, hauled*
calm	*k.a.m.*	cab, calm, cam, cap, carp, gap, ham, harm, harp
calves	*k.a.v.s.*	calves, halves, *carved*
cam	*k.a.m.*	cab, calm, cam, cap, carp, gap, ham, harm, harp
came	*k.ay.m.*	came, game
can	*k.a.t.*	can, card, cart, cat, guard, had, hard, hat, heart
candle	*k.a.t.t.l.*	candle, handle
candles	*k.a.t.t.l.s.*	candles, handles, *handled*
candour	*k.a.t.t.aw.*	candour, *condor, contour*

cane	*k.ay.t.*	cane, gain, gait, gate, hate
cannon	*k.a.t.o.t.*	cannon, cannot
cannot	*k.a.t.o.t.*	cannon, cannot
can't	*k.a.t.t.*	can't, hadn't, hand
cap	*k.a.m.*	cab, calm, cam, cap, carp, gap, ham, harm, harp
caped	*k.ay.m.t.*	caped, gaped, *caned, gained*
card	*k.a.t.*	can, card, cart, cat, guard, had, hard, hat, heart
cards	*k.a.t.s.*	cards, cats, guards, hands, harts, hats, hearts
care	*k.air.*	care, hair, hare
career	*k.a.r.ear.*	career, carrier
careless	*k.air.l.e.s.*	careless, hairless
carp	*k.a.m.*	cab, calm, cam, cap, carp, gap, ham, harm, harp
carriage	*k.a.r.i.j.*	carriage, garage
carrier	*k.a.r.ear.*	career, carrier
cars	*k.a.s.*	cars, gas, has
cart	*k.a.t.*	can, card, cart, cat, guard, had, hard, hat, heart

carved

carved	*k.a.v.t.*	carved, *calves, halves*
carving	*k.a.v.i.ng.*	carving, having
case	*k.ay.s.*	case, gaze, haze
cash	*k.a.j.*	cadge, cash, hash, hatch
cat	*k.a.t.*	can, card, cart, cat, guard, had, hard, hat, heart
catch	*k.a.j.*	cadge, cash, hash, hatch
cats	*k.a.t.s.*	cards, cats, guards, hands, harts, hats, hearts
caught	*k.aw.t.*	caught, chord, cord, corn, court, horn, hourd
cause	*k.aw.s.*	cause, coarse, course, horse
cautious	*k.aw.j.us*	gorgeous, cautious
cave	*k.ay.v.*	cave, gave
cease	*s.ee.s.*	cease, sees, seize
ceased	*s.ee.s.t.*	ceased, seized, *season, seasoned*
ceasing	*s.ee.s.i.ng.*	ceasing, seizing
cede	*s.ee.t.*	cede, scene, seat, seed, seen
cell	*s.e.l.*	cell, sell
cellars	*s.e.l.er.s.*	cellars, sellers
cells	*s.e.l.s.*	cells, sells
cent	*s.e.t.t.*	cent, scent, send, sent

chain	*j.ay.t.*	chase, chased, chain, shade
chained	*j.ay.t.t.*	chained, *chains*
chains	*j.ay.t.s.*	chains, *chained*
chair	*j.air.*	chair, share
chairs	*j.air.s.*	chairs, shares, *shared*
chaise	*j.ay.s.*	chase, chased, chain, shade
chance	*j.a.t.s.*	chance, charts
chap	*j.a.m.*	chap, charm, jab, jam, sham, sharp
charm	*j.a.m.*	chap, charm, jab, jam, sham, sharp
charmed	*j.a.m.t.*	charmed, jammed
charts	*j.a.t.s.*	chance, charts
chase	*j.ay.s.*	chase, chased, chain, shade
chased	*j.ay.s.t.*	chase, chased, chain, shade
chasm	*k.a.s.m.*	chasm, gasp
cheap	*j.ee.m.*	cheap, sheep
cheat	*j.ee.t.*	cheese, cheat, sheet, jean, sheet
cheats	*j.ee.t.s.*	jeans, sheets, cheats
check	*j.e.k.*	check, cheque
cheer	*j.ear.*	cheer, jeer, shear, sheer

cheered

cheered	*j.ear.t.*	shears, jeered
cheese	*j.ee.s.*	cheese, cheat, sheet, jean, sheet
cheque	*j.e.k.*	check, cheque
cherry	*j.e.r.ee.*	cherry, sherry
chin	*j.i.t.*	chin, gin
chip	*j.i.m.*	chip, Jim, gym, ship
chipped	*j.i.m.t.*	chips, chipped, ships, shipped
chips	*j.i.m.s.*	chips, chipped, ships, shipped
choir	*w.ii.er.*	choir, wire
choirs	*k.w.ii.er.*	choirs, wires
choke	*j.oh.k.*	joke, choke
choked	*j.oh.k.t.*	choked, chokes, jokes
choose	*j.oo.s.*	choose, juice, shoes
chop	*j.o.m.*	chop, job, shop
chopping	*j.o.m.i.ng.*	chopping, shopping
chops	*j.o.m.s.*	chops, jobs
chord	*k.aw.t.*	caught, chord, cord, corn, court, horn, hourd
chore	*j.aw.*	chore, jaw, shore
chore	*j.aw.*	chore, jaw, shore
chores	*j.aw.s.*	chores, jaws, shores
chose	*j.oh.s.*	chose, shows

cited	s.ii.t.i.t.	cited, sided, sighted, sited
citing	s.ii.t.i.ng.	citing siding, sighning, sighting, siting
clamp	k.l.a.m.m.	clamp, *clap*
clamp	k.l.a.m.m.	clamp, *clap*
clamped	k.l.a.m.m.t.	clamped, *clapped*
clamping	k.l.a.m.m.i.ng.	clamping, *clapping*
clap	k.l.a.m.	clap, *clamp*
clapped	k.l.a.m.t.	clapped, *clamped*
clapping	k.l.a.m.i.ng.	clapping, *clamping*
class	k.l.a.s.	class, glass
classes	k.l.a.s.e.s.	classes, glasses
cline	k.l.ii.t.	cline, glide
clips	k.l.i.m.s.	clips, glimpse
clock	k.l.o.k.	clock, clog
clocks	k.l.o.k.s.	clocks, clogs
clog	k.l.o.k.	clog, clock
clogs	k.l.o.k.s.	clogs, clocks
close	k.l.oh.s.	close, glows
club	k.l.u.m.	club, *clump*
clubs	k.l.u.m.s.	clubs, *clumps*
clump	k.l.u.m.m.	clump, *club*

clumps

clumps	k.l.u.m.m.s.	clumps, *clubs*
coal	k.oh.l.	coal, goal, hole, whole
coals	k.oh.l.s.	coals, goals, holes
coarse	k.aw.s.	cause, coarse, course, horse
coast	k.oh.s.t.	coast, coaxed, ghost, host
coasting	k.oh.s.t.i.ng.	coasting, hosting
coat	k.oh.t.	coat, code, cone, goad
coats	k.oh.t.s.	coats, goats, goads
coaxed	k.oh.s.t.	coast, coaxed, ghost, host
cock	k.o.k.	cock, hog
cod	k.o.t.	cod, cot, god, gone, got, hod, hot, *odd, on*
code	k.oh.t.	coat, code, cone, goad
coffee	k.o.v.ee.	coffee, *toffee, copy*
coffer	k.o.v.er.	coffer, hover, *cover*
cold	k.oh.l.t.	cold, gold, hold, holed
coley	k.oh.l.ee.	coley, holy, wholly
come	k.u.m.	come, cup, gum, hub, hum
comes	k.u.m.s.	comes, cups, gums, hubs, hums
comma	k.o.m.u.	comma, copper, hopper
complained	k.o.m.m.l.ay.t.t.	complained, complaint

complaint	*k.o.m.m.l.ay.t.t.*	complaint, complained
composed	*k.o.m.m.oh.s.t.*	composed, *compost*
compost	*k.o.m.m.o.s.t.*	compost, *composed*
concede	*k.o.t.s.ee.t.*	concede, conceit
conceded	*k.o.t.s.ee.t.e.t.*	conceded, conceited
conceit	*k.o.t.s.ee.t.*	concede, conceit
conceited	*k.o.t.s.ee.t.i.t.*	conceded, conceited
concern	*k.o.t.s.er.t.t.*	concern, concert, *concerned*
concerned	*k.o.t.s.er.t.t.*	concerned, *concern, consert*
concerns	*k.o.t.s.er.t.s.*	concerns, concerts
concert	*k.o.t.s.er.t.*	concern, concert, *concerned*
concerts	*k.o.t.s.er.t.s.*	concerns, concerts
condor	*k.o.t.t.aw.*	condor, *candour, contour*
cone	*k.oh.t.*	coat, code, cone, goad
consent	*k.o.t.s.e.t.t.*	consent, godsend
contend	*k.o.t.t.e.t.t.*	contend, content
contended	*k.o.t.t.e.t.t.e.t.*	contended, contented
content	*k.o.t.t.e.t.t.*	contend, content
contented	*k.o.t.t.e.t.t.e.t.*	contended, contented
convict	*k.o.t.v.i.k.t.*	convict, *convince*
cook	*k.uu.k.*	cook, hook

cooked

cooked	*k.uu.k.t.*	cooked, hooked
cope	*k.oh.m.*	home, hope, cope
copper	*k.o.m.er.*	comma, copper, hopper
copy	*k.o.m.ee.*	copy, coffee, toffee
cord	*k.aw.t.*	caught, chord, cord, corn, court, horn, hourd
corn	*k.aw.t.*	caught, chord, cord, corn, court, horn, hourd
cornered	*k.aw.t.er.t.*	cornered, *corners*
corners	*k.aw.t.er.s.*	corners, *cornered*
cornet	*k.aw.t.i.t.*	cornet, hoarded
corresponded	*k.o.r.e.s.m.o.t.t.e.t.*	correspondent, corresponded
correspondent	*k.o.r.e.s.m.o.t.t.t.t.*	correspondent, corresponded
cot	*k.o.t.*	cod, cot, god, gone, got, hod, hot, *odd, on*
cots	*k.o.t.s.*	cots, gods, hods
could	*k.uu.t.*	could, good, hood
count	*k.ow.t.t.*	count, gowned, hound
course	*k.aw.s.*	cause, coarse, course, horse
court	*k.aw.t.*	caught, chord, cord, corn, court, horn, hourd
cover	*k.u.v.er.*	cover, *hover, coffer*
cow	*k.ow.*	cow, how

cower	*k.ow.er.*	cower, *hour, our*
cowl	*k.ow.l.*	cowl, *owl*
cows	*k.ow.s.*	cows, house
crab	*k.r.a.m.*	crab, cram, grab, gram
cram	*k.r.a.m.*	crab, cram, grab, gram
crane	*k.r.ay.t.*	crane, crate, grade, grain, grate, great,
crate	*k.r.ay.t.*	crane, crate, grade, grain, grate, great,
creak	*k.r.ee.k.*	creak, creek, Greek
cream	*k.r.ee.m.*	cream, creep
creek	*k.r.ee.k.*	creak, creek, Greek
creep	*k.r.ee.m.*	cream, creep
crew	*k.r.oo.*	crew, grew
crib	*k.r.i.m.*	crib, grim, grip
crime	*k.r.ii.m.*	crime, *rhyme, rime, ripe*
crow	*k.r.oh.*	crow, grow
crowd	*k.r.ow.t.*	crowd, crown, grout
crowding	*k.r.ow.t.i.ng.*	crowding, crowning, grouting
crown	*k.r.ow.t.*	crowd, crown, grout
crowned	*k.r.ow.t.t.*	crowned, ground
crowning	*k.r.ow.t.i.ng.*	crowding, crowning, grouting
crows	*k.r.oh.s.*	crows, grows

crumbs

crumbs	*k.r.u.m.s.*	crumbs, grubs
crush	*k.r.u.j.*	crush, crutch, grudge
crushed	*k.r.u.j.t.*	crushed, crutched
crushing	*k.r.u.j.i.ng.*	crushing, grudging
crutch	*k.r.u.j.*	crush, crutch, grudge
crutched	*k.r.u.j.t.*	crushed, crutched
cud	*k.u.t.*	cut, cud, gun, gut, hut
cunning	*k.u.t.i.ng.*	cunning, cutting, gutting
cup	*k.u.m.*	come, cup, gum, hub, hum
cups	*k.u.m.s.*	comes, cups, gums, hubs, hums
curb	*k.er.m.*	curb, herb, *verb, blurb*
curly	*k.er.l.ee.*	curly, girly, *early*
currant	*k.u.r.uu.t.t.*	currant, current
current	*k.u.r.e.t.t.*	currant, current
curry	*k.u.r.ee.*	curry, hurry
Curse	*K.er.s.*	curse, hers
curt	*k.er.t.*	curt, gird, gurn, heard, herd, hurt
cut	*k.u.t.*	cut, cud, gun, gut, hut
cuts	*k.u.t.s.*	cuts, guns, guts, huts
cutting	*k.u.t.i.ng.*	cunning, cutting, gutting

dab	*t.a.m.*	dab, dam, damn, damp, nab, nap, tab, tamp, tap
dabbed	*t.a.m.t.*	dabbed, dammed, damned,damped, knapped, nabbed, napped, tabbed, tamped, tapped
dabbing	*t.a.m.i.ng.*	dabbing, damming, nabbing, napping, tabbing, tamping, tapping, *napkin*
dabs	*t.a.m.s.*	dabs, dams, nabs, naps, tabs, tamps, taps
daddy	*t.a.t.ee.*	daddy, dandy, natty, tatty, *darted, tarded, tanzy*
dale	*t.ay.l.*	dale, nail, tail, tale, *snail, stale*
dales	*t.ay.t.s.*	dales, nails, tails, tales, *snails*
dam	*t.a.m.*	dab, dam, damn, damp, nab, nap, tab, tamp, tap
dame	*t.ay.m.*	dame, name, nape, tame, tape
dames	*t.ay.m.s.*	dames, names, napes, tames, tapes
dammed	*t.a.m.t.*	dabbed, dammed, damned,damped, knapped, nabbed, napped, tabbed, tamped, tapped

damming

damming	*t.a.m.i.ng.*	dabbing, damming, nabbing, napping, tabbing, tamping, tapping, *napkin*
damn	*t.a.m.*	dab, dam, damn, damp, nab, nap, tab, tamp, tap
damned	*t.a.m.t.*	dabbed, dammed, damned,damped, knapped, nabbed, napped, tabbed, tamped, tapped
damp	*t.a.m.m.*	dab, dam, damn, damp, nab, nap, tab, tamp, tap
damped	*t.a.m.m.t.*	dabbed, dammed, damned,damped, knapped, nabbed, napped, tabbed, tamped, tapped
dams	*t.a.m.s.*	dabs, dams, nabs, naps, tabs, tamps, taps
dance	*t.a.t.s.*	dance, darts, tarts,*stance*
dances	*t.a.t.s.e.s.*	dances, *stances*
dandy	*t.a.t.t.ee.*	daddy, dandy, natty, tatty, *darted, tarded, tanzy*
dane	*t.ay.t.*	dane, date
dangle	*t.a.ng.k.l.*	dangle, tangle
dangled	*t.a.ng.k.l.t.*	dangled, tangled
dangling	*t.a.ng.l.i.ng.*	dangling, tangling
dare	*t.air.*	dare, tear, tare

dark	*t.a.k.*	dark, nark
darken	*t.a.k.e.t.*	darken, target
darn	*t.a.t.*	darn, dart, tarn, tarred, tart, *tan, tat*
dart	*t.a.t.*	darn, dart, tarn, tarred, tart, *tan, tat*
darted	*t.a.t.e.t.*	darted, tarded, *daddy, dandy, natty, tatty*
darts	*t.a.t.s.*	dance, darts, tarts,*stance*
date	*t.ay.t.*	dane, date
dative	*t.ay.t.i.v.*	dative, native
dawn	*t.aw.t.*	dawn, gnawed, nought, torn, tort, toured, taught
dawning	*t.aw.t.i.ng.*	dawning, *taunting*
day	*t.ay.*	day, neigh, TAY
dead	*t.e.t.*	dead, debt, den, net, ten, *dent,tent*
deaf	*t.e.v.*	deaf, *death*
deafened	*t.e.v.uu.t.t.*	deafened, *defence, defends*
deal	*t.ee.l.*	deal, kneel
dealer	*t.ee.l.er.*	dealer, kneeler
dealing	*t.ee.l.i.ng.*	dealing, kneeling
dealt	*t.e.l.t.*	dealt, geld, knelt
dean	*t.ee.t.*	dean, deed, neat, need, teat, teen

deans

deans	*t.ee.t.s.*	deans, deeds, needs, teats, teens
dear	*t.ear.*	dear, deer, near, tear
dear	*t.ear.*	dear, near, tear
dearer	*t.ear.r.er.*	dearer, nearer
dearest	*t.ear.r.e.s.t.*	dearest, nearest
death	*t.e.th.*	death, *deaf*
debt	*t.e.t.*	dead, debt, den, net, ten, *dent,tent*
debts	*t.e.t.s.*	debts, dense, tense,*dents, tents*
decide	*t.e.s.ii.t.*	decide, design
decides	*t.e.s.ii.t.s.*	decides, designs,
deck	*t.e.k.*	deck, neck
decree	*t.e.k.r.ee.*	decree, degree
decrees	*t.e.k.r.ee.s.*	decrees, degrees
deed	*t.ee.t.*	dean, deed, neat, need, teat, teen
deeds	*t.ee.t.s.*	deans, deeds, needs, teats, teens
deem	*t.ee.m.*	deem, deep, neap, team
deemed	*t.ee.m.t.*	deemed, teamed, teemed
deems	*t.ee.m.s.*	deems, deeps, teams, teems
deep	*t.ee.m.*	deem, deep, neap, team

deeps	*t.ee.m.s.*	deems, deeps, teams, teems
deer	*t.ear.*	dear, deer, near, tear
defence	*t.e.v.e.t.s.*	defence, defends, *deafened*
defends	*t.i.v.e.t.t.s.*	defence, defends, *deafened*
define	*t.e.v.ii.t.*	define, *design*
degree	*t.e.k.r.ee.*	decree, degree
degrees	*t.e.k.r.ee.s.*	decrees, degrees
dell	*t.e.l.t.*	dell, tell
den	*t.e.t.*	dead, debt, den, net, ten, *dent,tent*
dense	*t.e.t.s.*	debts, dense, tense,*dents, tents*
dent	*t.e.t.t.*	dent, tent, *dead, debt, den, net, ten*
denting	*t.e.t.t.i.ng.*	denting, tending, tenting
dents	*t.e.t.t.s.*	dents, tents, *debts, dense, tense*
descend	*t.i.s.e.t.t.*	descend, descent
descent	*t.i.s.e.t.t.*	descend, descent
desert	*t.e.s.er.t.*	desert, dessert, discern
design	*t.e.s.ii.t.*	decide, design
designs	*t.e.s.ii.t.s.*	decides, designs,
dessert	*t.e.s.er.t.*	desert, dessert, discern

deuce

deuce	*t.ew.s.*	deuce, news, *newts*
dew	*t.ew.*	dew, due, knew, new
dhow	*t.ow.*	dhow, now
dial	*t.ii.u.l.*	dial, tile
dialled	*t.ii.uu.l.t.*	dialled, tiled
dials	*t.ii.uu.l.s.*	dials, tiles
dib	*t.i.m.*	dib, dim, dip, nib, nip, TIM, tip
dibbed	*t.i.m.t.*	dibbed, dimmed, dipped, nibbed, nipped, tipped,
dibber	*t.i.m.er.*	dibber, dimmer, dipper, nipper, timber, tipper
dibs	*t.i.m.s.*	dips, dims, dips, nibs, nips, tips
dice	*t.ii.s.*	dice, dyes, nice, ties
DICK	*T.I.K.*	DICK, dig, nick, tick, tig
did	*t.i.t.*	did, din, dint, knit, nit, tin, *didn't*
didn't	*t.i.t.t.*	didn't, *did, din, knit, nit, tin*
die	*t.ii.*	die, nigh, tie
died	*t.ii.t.*	died, dine, dined, dyed, knight, night, nine, tide, tied, tight, tine
dig	*t.i.k.*	DICK, dig, nick, tick, tig
dig it	*t.i.k. i.t.*	dig it, nick it, ticket

digger	*t.i.k.er.*	dicker, nicker, nigger, ticker
digging	*t.i.k.i.ng.*	digging, nicking, ticking
digs	*t.i.k.s.*	digs, nicks, ticks
dill	*t.i.l.*	dill, nil, till
dim	*t.i.m.*	dib, dim, dip, nib, nip, TIM, tip
dimly	*t.i.m.l.ee.*	dimly, *nimbly*
dimmed	*t.i.m.t.*	dibbed, dimmed, dipped, nibbed, nipped, tipped,
dimmer	*t.i.m.er.*	dibber, dimmer, dipper, nipper, timber, tipper
dimple	*t.i.m.m.uu.l.*	dimple, nimble, nipple, tipple
dimples	*t.i.m.m.l.s.*	dimples, nipples, tipples
dims	*t.i.m.s.*	dips, dims, dips, nibs, nips, tips
din	*t.i.t.*	did, din, dint, knit, nit, tin, *didn't*
dine	*t.ii.t.*	died, dine, dined, dyed, knight, night, nine, tide, tied, tight, tine
dined	*t.ii.t.t.*	died, dine, dined, dyed, knight, night, nine, tide, tied, tight, tine
dines	*t.ii.t.s.*	dines, knights, nights, nines, tides, tights, tines

dint

dint	*t.i.t.t.*	did, din, dint, knit, nit, tin, *didn't*
dip	*t.i.m.*	dib, dim, dip, nib, nip, TIM, tip
dipped	*t.i.m.t.*	dibbed, dimmed, dipped, nibbed, nipped, tipped,
dipper	*t.i.m.er.*	dibber, dimmer, dipper, nipper, timber, tipper
dips	*t.i.m.s.*	dips, dims, dips, nibs, nips, tips
dire	*t.ii.er.*	dire, tire, tyre
dirt	*t.er.t.*	dirt, nerd, turd, turn
dirts	*t.er.t.s.*	dirts, turds, turns
discern	*t.i.s.er.t.*	desert, dessert, discern
dish	*t.i.j.*	dish, ditch, niche, titch
dishes	*t.i.j.e.s.*	dished, ditches, titches
dismay	*t.i.s.m.ay.*	dismay, *display, disobey*
dismays	*t.i.s.m.ay.s.*	dismays, *disobeys, displays*
disobey	*t.i.s.oh.m.ay.*	disobey, *dismay, display*
disobeys	*t.i.s.oh.m.ay.s.*	disobeys, *dismays, displays*
display	*t.i.s.m.l.ay.*	display, *dismay, disobey*
displays	*t.i.s.m.l.ay.s.*	displays, *dismays, disobeys*
ditch	*t.i.j.*	dish, ditch, niche, titch

ditches	*t.i.j.e.s.*	dished, ditches, titches
dive	*t.ii.v.*	dive, knife
dives	*t.ii.v.s.*	dives, knives
do	*t.oo.*	do, to, too, two
dob	*t.o.m.*	dob, knob, nob, TOM, top
dobbed	*t.o.m.t.*	dobbed, knobbed, topped
dock	*t.o.k.*	dock, dog, knock, nog, tog
docks	*t.o.k.s.*	docks, dogs, knocks, nogs, togs
dodged	*t.o.j.t.*	dodged, notched
doe	*t.oh.*	doe, dough, know, no, toe, tow, *toad, tone*
doesn't	*t.u.s.uu.t.t.*	doesn't, dozen, dust
dog	*t.o.k.*	dock, dog, knock, nog, tog
dogs	*t.o.k.s.*	docks, dogs, knocks, nogs, togs
doll	*t.o.l.*	doll, knoll, toll
dome	*t.oh.m.*	dome, dope, gnome, tome
don	*t.o.t.*	don, dot, knot, nod, non, not, tot
done	*t.u.t.*	done, dud, none, nut, tonne, ton

donor

donor	*t.oh.t.er.*	donor, toner
dons	*t.o.t.s.*	dons, dots, knots, nods, tots
doom	*t.oo.m.*	doom, tomb
dooms	*t.oo.m.s.*	dooms, tombs
door	*t.aw.*	door, gnaw, nor, tore, tour
doors	*t.aw.s.*	doors, gnaws, tours
dope	*t.oh.m.*	dome, dope, gnome, tome
dosed	*t.oh.s.t.*	dosed, dozed, toast
doss	*t.o.s.*	doss, toss
dossed	*t.o.s.t.*	dossed, tossed
dossing	*t.o.s.i.ng.*	dossing, tossing
dot	*t.o.t.*	don, dot, knot, nod, non, not, tot
doted	*t.oh.t.e.t.*	doted, noted
dotes	*t.oh.t.s.*	dotes, nodes, notes, toads, tones
dots	*t.o.t.s.*	dons, dots, knots, nods, tots
doubt	*t.ow.t.*	doubt, down, noun, nowt, town
doubts	*t.ow.t.s.*	doubts, downs, nouns,toutes, towns

dough	*t.oh.*	doe, dough, know, no, toe, tow, *toad, tone, towed*
dove	*t.u.v.*	dove, tough
dowel	*t.ow.uu.l.*	dowel, towel
dower	*t.ow.er.*	dower, tower
down	*t.ow.t.*	doubt, down, noun, nowt, town
downs	*t.ow.t.s.*	doubts, downs, nouns, toutes, towns
doze	*t.oh.s.*	doze, knows, nose, toes
dozed	*t.oh.s.t.*	dosed, dozed, toast
dozen	*t.u.s.t.*	doesn't, dozen, dust
dozes	*t.oh.s.i.s.*	dozes, noses
drab	*t.r.a.m.*	drab, dram, tram, tramp, trap
drag	*t.r.a.k.*	drag, track
dragged	*t.r.a.k.t.*	dragged, tracked
dragging	*t.r.a.k.i.ng.*	dragging, tracking
drags	*t.r.a.k.s.*	drags, tracks
drain	*t.r.ay.t.*	drain, trade, train, trait
drained	*t.r.ay.t.t.*	drained, trained
drainer	*t.r.ay.t.er.*	drainer, trader, trainer, traitor
draining	*t.r.ay.t.i.ng.*	draining, trading, training

drains

drains	*t.r.ay.t.s.*	drains, trades, trains, traits
dram	*t.r.a.m.*	drab, dram, tram, tramp, trap
drama	*t.r.a.m.u.*	drama, *trauma*
drams	*t.r.a.m.s.*	drams, trams, tramps, traps
drawler	*t.r.aw.l.er.*	drawler, trawler
drawling	*t.r.aw.l.i.ng.*	drawl, trawl
drawling	*t.r.aw.l.i.ng.*	drawling, trawling
dray	*t.r.ay.*	dray, tray
dread	*t.r.e.t.*	dread, tread
dreads	*t.r.e.t.s.*	dreads, treads, trends
dregs	*t.r.e.k.s.*	dregs, treks
dress	*t.r.e.s.*	dress, tress
dresses	*t.r.e.s.i.s.*	dresses, tresses
drew	*t.r.oo.*	drew, true
dried	*t.r.ii.t.*	dried, tried
drier	*t.r.ii.er.*	dryer, tryer
drill	*t.r.i.l.*	drill, trill
drip	*t.r.i.m.*	drip, trim, trip
dripped	*t.r.i.m.t.*	dripped, trimmed, tripped
dripping	*t.r.i.m.i.ng.*	dripping, trimming, tripping

drips	*t.r.i.m.s.*	drips, trims, trips
droll	*t.r.o.l.*	droll, troll
droop	*t.room.*	droop, troop
drooped	*t.r.oo.m.t.*	drooped, trooped
droops	*t.r.oo.m.s.*	droops, troops, troupes
drove	*t.r.oh.v.*	drove, trove
drown	*t.r.ow.t.*	drown trout
drub	*t.r.u.m.*	drub, drum
drudge	*t.r.u.j.*	drudge, trudge
drug	*t.r.u.k.*	drug, truck
drugs	*t.r.u.k.s.*	drugs, trucks
drum	*t.r.u.m.*	drub, drum
drunk	*t.r.u.ng.k.*	drunk, trunk
drunks	*t.r.u.ng.k.s.*	drunks, trunks
dry	*t.r.ii.*	dry, try
drying	*t.r.ii.i.ng.*	drying, trying
duck	*t.u.k.*	duck, dug, tuck, tug
ducked	*t.u.k.t.*	ducked, tucked
ducking	*t.u.k.i.ng.*	ducking, tucking, *dunking*
dud	*t.u.t.*	done, dud, none, nut, tonne, ton
duds	*t.u.t.s.*	duds, nuns, nuts, tonnes, tons

due

due	*t.ew.*	dew, due, knew, new
dug	*t.u.k.*	duck, dug, tuck, tug
dull	*t.u.l.*	dull, null
duly	*t.ew.l.ee.*	duly, newly
dumb	*t.u.m.*	dumb, numb, tub, *dump*
dumbed	*t.u.m.t.*	dumbed, numbed
dump	*t.u.m.m.*	dump, *dumb, numb, tub*
dumper	*t.u.m.m.er.*	dumper, number
dumpers	*t.u.m.m.er.s.*	dumpers, numbers
dune	*t.oo.t.*	dune, *nude, newt, tune*
dung	*t.u.ng.*	dung, tongue, *dunk*
dunk	*t.u.ng.k.*	dunk, *dung, tongue*
dunking	*t.u.ng.k.i.ng.*	dunking, *ducking, tucking*
dusk	*t.u.s.k.*	dusk, tusk
dust	*t.u.s.t.*	doesn't, dozen, dust
dustman	*t.u.s.m.a.t.*	dustman, dustpan
dustpan	*t.u.s.m.a.t.*	dustman, dustpan
dutch	*t.u.j.*	dutch, touch
dyed	*t.ii.t.*	died, dine, dined, dyed, knight, night, nine, tide, tied, tight, tine
dyes	*t.ii.s.*	dice, dyes, nice, ties
dying	*t.ii.i.ng.*	dying, tying

early	*er.l.ee.*	early, *curly, girly*
earn	*er.t.*	earn, urn
ebb	*e.m.*	ebb, em
eddy	*e.t.ee.*	any, eddy
edge	*e.j.*	edge, *hedge, age*
edged	*e.j.t.*	edged, etched
eggs	*e.k.s.*	eggs, *ex*
eight	*ay.t.*	aid, ate, eight, *gate, hate, Kate*
eighteen	*ay.t.ee.t.*	eighteen, *eighty*
eighty	*ay.t.ee.*	eighty, *eighteen*
em	*e.m.*	ebb, em
ex	*e.k.s.*	ex, *eggs*
except	*e.s.e.m.t.*	except, exempt, *accept*
exempt	*e.s.e.m.t.*	except, exempt, *accept*
expands	*e.s.m.a.t.t.s.*	expands, *expanse*
expanse	*e.s.m.a.t.s.*	expanse, *expands*
expel	*e.s.m.e.l.*	expel, *smell, spell*
extend	*e.s.t.e.t.t.*	extend, extent
extent	*e.s.t.e.t.t.*	extend, extent
eyes	*ii.s.*	eyes, ice, *highs*
fad	*v.a.t.*	fad, fan, fat, van, vat

fade

fade	*v.ay.t.*	fade, fate, feign, fete, vain, vein, *faint*
fail	*v.ay.l.*	fail, veil
faint	*v.ay.t.t.*	faint, feigned, *fade, fate, feign, fete, vain, vein*
fair	*v.air.*	fair, fare
fairy	*v.air.r.ee.*	fairy, vary
falls	*v.aw.l.s.*	falls, false
false	*v.aw.l.s.*	falls, false
fan	*v.a.t.*	fad, fan, fat, van, vat
fare	*v.air.*	fair, fare
farther	*v.a.th.er.*	farther, father
fast	*v.a.s.t.*	fast, vast
faster	*v.a.s.t.er.*	faster, vaster
fastest	*v.a.s.t.e.s.t.*	fastest, vastest
fat	*v.a.t.*	fad, fan, fat, van, vat
fate	*v.ay.t.*	fade, fate, feign, fete, vain, vein, *faint*
father	*v.a.th.er.*	farther, father
fault	*v.aw.l.t.*	fault, vault
faults	*v.aw.l.t.s.*	faults, vaults
fawned	*v.aw.t.t.*	fought, fawned
fear	*v.ear.*	fear, veer
feared	*v.ear.t.*	feared, veered

fearing	*v.ear.r.i.ng.*	fearing, veering
fears	*v.ear.s.*	fears, veers
feat	*v.ee.t.*	feat, feed, feet
feats	*v.ee.t.s.*	feats, feeds
fed	*v.e.t.*	fed, fen, vet, *fend*
feed	*v.ee.t.*	feat, feed, feet
feeds	*v.ee.t.s.*	feats, feeds
feel	*v.ee.l.*	feel, veal
feet	*v.ee.t.*	feat, feed, feet
feign	*v.ay.t.*	fade, fate, feign, fete, vain, vein, *faint*
feigned	*v.ay.t.t.*	faint, feigned, *fade, fate, feign, fete, vain, vein*
felled	*v.e.l.t.*	felled, felt
felt	*v.e.l.t.*	felled, felt
fen	*v.e.t.*	fed, fen, vet, *fend*
fend	*v.e.t.t.*	fend, *fed, fen, vet*
fender	*v.e.t.t.er.*	fender, *vendor*
ferry	*v.e.r.ee.*	ferry, very
fetch	*v.e.j.*	fetch, vetch
fete	*v.ay.t.*	fade, fate, feign, fete, vain, vein, *faint*
few	*v.ew.*	few, view
fez	*v.e.s.*	fez, vex

fiction

fiction	*v.i.k.j.u.t.*	fiction, *fission, vision*
fifteen	*v.i.v.t.ee.t.*	fifteen, *fifty*
fifty	*v.i.v.t.ee.*	fifty, *fifteen*
fight	*v.ii.t.*	fight, find, fine, fined, vine, vined
fighter	*v.ii.t.er.*	fighter, finder, finer
fights	*v.ii.t.s.*	fights, fines, vines, *finds*
figs	*v.i.k.s.*	figs, fix
figure	*v.i.k.er.*	figure, vigour
file	*v.ii.l.*	file, vial, vile
files	*v.ii.l.s.*	files, vials
fin	*v.i.t.*	fin, fit
final	*v.ii.t.l.*	final, vital
find	*v.ii.t.t.*	fight, find, fine, fined, vine, vined
finder	*v.ii.t.t.er.*	fighter, finder, finer
finding	*v.ii.t.t.i.ng.*	finding, *fining*
finds	*v.ii.t.t.s.*	finds, *fights, fines, vines*
finds	*v.ii.t.t.s.*	finds, *fights, fines, vines*
fine	*v.ii.t.*	fight, find, fine, fined, vine, vined
fined	*v.ii.t.t.*	fight, find, fine, fined, vine, vined
finer	*v.ii.t.er.*	fighter, finder, finer
fins	*v.i.t.s.*	fins, fits

firm	*v.er.m.*	firm, verb
first	*v.er.s.t.*	first, versed, *verse*
fission	*v.i.j.u.t.*	fission, vision, *fiction*
fist	*v.i.s.t.*	fist, fixed, fizzed
fit	*v.i.t.*	fin, fit
fits	*v.i.t.s.*	fins, fits
fix	*v.i.s.*	figs, fix
fix	*v.i.s.*	fix, fizz
fixed	*v.i.s.t.*	fist, fixed, fizzed
fizz	*v.i.s.*	fix, fizz
fizzed	*v.i.s.t.*	fist, fixed, fizzed
flab	*v.l.a.m.*	flab, flap
flack	*v.l.a.k.*	flack, flag
flag	*v.l.a.k.*	flack, flag
flan	*v.l.a.t.*	flan, flat
flap	*v.l.a.m.*	flab, flap
flat	*v.l.a.t.*	flan, flat
fleas	*v.l.ee.s.*	fleas, fleece
fleece	*v.l.ee.s.*	fleas, fleece
flint	*v.l.i.t.t.*	flit, flint
flit	*v.l.i.t.*	flit, flint
float	*v.l.oh.t.*	float, flowed, flown

flock

flock	*v.l.o.k.*	flock, flog
flog	*v.l.o.k.*	flock, flog
flour	*v.l.ow.er.*	flour, flower
flowed	*v.l.oh.t.*	float, flowed, flown
flower	*v.l.ow.er.*	flour, flower
flown	*v.l.oh.t.*	float, flowed, flown
foe	*v.oh.*	foe, *folk, vogue*
foes	*v.oh.s.*	foes, *folks*
folk	*v.oh.k.*	folk, vogue, *foe*
folks	*v.oh.k.s.*	folks, *foes*
folly	*v.o.l.ee.*	folly, volley
fond	*v.o.t.t.*	fond, font
font	*v.o.t.t.*	fond, font
for	*v.aw.*	for, four, *fork*
foregone	*v.aw.k.o.t.*	foregone, forgot
forehead	*v.aw.k.e.t.*	forehead, forget
forget	*v.aw.k.e.t.*	forehead, forget
forgot	*v.aw.k.o.t.*	foregone, forgot
fork	*v.aw.k.*	fork, *for, four*
forth	*v.aw.th.*	forth, fourth
fought	*v.aw.t.*	fought, fawned
foul	*v.ow.l.*	foul, fowl, vowel
found	*v.ow.t.t.*	found, fount

fount	*v.ow.t.t.*	found, fount
four	*v.aw.*	for, four, *fork*
fourth	*v.aw.th.*	forth, fourth
fowl	*v.ow.l.*	foul, fowl, vowel
fowls	*v.ow.l.s.*	fowls, vowels
fraud	*v.r.aw.t.*	fraud, fraught
fraught	*v.r.aw.t.*	fraud, fraught
frayed	*v.r.ay.t.*	frayed, freight
FRED	*V.R.E.T.*	FRED, fret, friend
freight	*v.r.ay.t.*	frayed, freight
fret	*v.r.e.t.*	FRED, fret, friend
fried	*v.r.ii.t.*	fried, fright
friend	*v.r.e.t.t.*	FRED, fret, friend
fright	*v.r.ii.t.*	fried, fright
frock	*v.r.o.k.*	frock, frog
frocks	*v.r.o.k.s.*	frocks, frogs
frog	*v.r.o.k.*	frock, frog
frogs	*v.r.o.k.s.*	frocks, frogs
fun	*v.u.t.*	fun, fund
fund	*v.u.t.t.*	fun, fund
fuse	*v.ew.s.*	fuse, views

gain

gain	*k.ay.t.*	cane, gain, gait, gate, hate
gained	*k.ay.t.t.*	gained, *gains, gates*
gains	*k.ay.t.s.*	gains, gates, *gained*
gait	*k.ay.t.*	cane, gain, gait, gate, hate
gales	*k.ay.l.s.*	gales, *hailed*
game	*k.ay.m.*	came, game
games	*k.ay.m.s.*	games, *caped*
gang	*k.a.ng.*	gang, hang
gangs	*k.a.ng.s.*	gangs, hanged
gap	*k.a.m.*	cab, calm, cam, cap, carp, gap, ham, harm, harp
garage	*k.a.r.i.j.*	carriage, garage
garden	*k.a.t.e.t.*	garden, guarded, hardened, hearted
gardened	*k.a.t.e.t.t.*	gardened, hardened
gardening	*k.a.t.e.t.i.ng.*	gardening, handing
gardens	*k.a.t.e.t.s.*	gardens, hardens
garment	*k.a.m.e.t.t.*	happens, garments
garments	*k.a.m.e.t.t.s.*	happens, garments
gas	*k.a.s.*	cars, gas, has
gasp	*k.a.s.m.*	chasm, gasp

gate	*k.ay.t.*	cane, gain, gait, gate, hate
gates	*k.ay.t.s.*	gains, gates, *gained*
gathered	*k.a.th.er.t.*	gathered, *gathers*
gathers	*k.a.th.er.s.*	gathers, *gathered*
gave	*k.ay.v.*	cave, gave
gay	*k.ay.*	gay, hay
gaze	*k.ay.s.*	case, gaze, haze
gazed	*k.ay.s.t.*	gazed, haste
gear	*k.ear.*	gear, hear, here
geese	*k.ee.s.*	geese, he's, keys, *heat, heed, keen, keyed*
geld	*k.e.l.t.*	dealt, geld, knelt
get	*k.e.t.*	get, head
gets	*k.e.t.s.*	gets, heads, hence
getting	*k.e.t.i.ng.*	getting,heading
ghost	*k.oh.s.t.*	coast, coaxed, ghost, host
giddy	*k.i.t.ee.*	giddy, guinea
gift	*k.i.v.t.*	gift, given, *gives*
gig	*k.i.k.*	gig, kick
gigs	*k.i.k.s.*	gigs, kicks
gill	*k.i.l.*	hill, kill, gill
gills	*k.i.l.s.*	gills, hills, kills

gin

gin	*j.i.t.*	chin, gin
gird	*k.er.t.*	curt, gird, gurn, heard, herd, hurt
girl	*k.er.l.*	curl, girl, hurl, *earl*
girls	*k.er.l.s.*	curls, curls, *earls*
given	*k.i.v.t.*	gift, given, *gives*
gives	*k.i.v.s.*	gives, *given, gift*
glass	*k.l.a.s.*	glass, class
glasses	*k.l.a.s.i.s.*	glasses, classes
glide	*k.l.ii.t.*	cline, glide
glimpse	*k.l.i.m.s.*	glimpse, clips
glows	*k.l.oh.s.*	glows, close
gnaw	*t.aw.*	door, gnaw, nor, tore, tour
gnawed	*t.aw.t.*	dawn, gnawed, nought, torn, tort, toured, taught
gnaws	*t.aw.s.*	doors, gnaws, tours
gnome	*t.oh.m.*	dome, dope, gnome, tome
go	*k.oh.*	go, hoe
goad	*k.oh.t.*	coat, code, cone, goad
goads	*k.oh.t.s.*	coats, goats, goads
goal	*k.oh.l.*	coal, goal, hole, whole
goals	*k.oh.l.s.*	coals, goals, holes
goats	*k.oh.t.s.*	coats, goats, goads

god	*k.o.t.*	cod, cot, god, gone, got, hod, hot, *odd, on*
gods	*k.o.t.s.*	cots, gods, hods
godsend	*k.o.t.s.e.t.t.*	consent, godsend
going	*k.oh.i.ng.*	going, hoeing, *owing*
gold	*k.oh.l.t.*	cold, gold, hold, holed
gone	*k.o.t.*	cod, cot, god, gone, got, hod, hot, *odd, on*
good	*k.uu.t.*	could, good, hood
gorgeous	*k.aw.j.u.s.*	gorgeous, cautious
got	*k.o.t.*	cod, cot, god, gone, got, hod, hot, *odd, on*
gout	*k.ow.t.*	gown, gout, *out*
gown	*k.ow.t.*	gown, gout, *out*
gowned	*k.ow.t.t.*	count, gowned, hound
grab	*k.r.a.m.*	crab, cram, grab, gram
grade	*k.r.ay.t.*	crane, crate, grade, grain, grate, great,
grader	*k.r.ay.t.er.*	grader, grater, greater
grain	*k.r.ay.t.*	crane, crate, grade, grain, grate, great,
gram	*k.r.a.m.*	crab, cram, grab, gram
grand	*k.r.a.t.t.*	grand, grant
grandma	*k.r.a.t.t.m.a.*	grandma, grandpa
grandpa	*k.r.a.t.t.m.a.*	grandma, grandpa

grant

grant	*k.r.a.t.t.*	grand, grant
grate	*k.r.ay.t.*	crane, crate, grade, grain, grate, great,
grater	*k.r.ay.t.er.*	grader, grater, greater
great	*k.r.ay.t.*	crane, crate, grade, grain, grate, great,
greater	*k.r.ay.t.er.*	grader, grater, greater
Greek	*K.r.ee.k.*	creak, creek, Greek
grew	*k.r.oo.*	crew, grew
grid	*k.r.i.t.*	grin, grit, grid
grief	*k.r.ee.v.*	grief, grieve
grieve	*k.r.ee.v.*	grief, grieve
grim	*k.r.i.m.*	crib, grim, grip
grin	*k.r.i.t.*	grin, grit, grid
grip	*k.r.i.m.*	crib, grim, grip
grit	*k.r.i.t.*	grin, grit, grid
groan	*k.r.oh.t.*	groan, grown
ground	*k.r.ow.t.t.*	crowned, ground
grout	*k.r.ow.t.*	crowd, crown, grout
grouting	*k.r.ow.t.i.ng.*	crowding, crowning, grouting
grow	*k.r.oh.*	crow, grow
grown	*k.r.oh.t.*	groan, grown
grows	*k.r.oh.s.*	crows, grows

grubs	*k.r.u.m.s.*	crumbs, grubs
grudge	*k.r.u.j.*	crush, crutch, grudge
grudging	*k.r.u.j.i.ng.*	crushing, grudging
Guard	*K.a.t.*	can, card, cart, cat, guard, had, hard, hat, heart
guarded	*k.a.t.e.t.*	garden, guarded, hardened, hearted
guards	*k.a.t.s.*	cards, cats, guards, hands, harts, hats, hearts
guide	*k.ii.t.*	guide, height, kite, *highs*
guiding	*k.ii.t.i.ng.*	guiding, hiding
guild	*k.i.l.t.*	guild, guilt, hilled, hilt, killed, kiln, kilt
guilt	*k.i.l.t.*	guild, guilt, hilled, hilt, killed, kiln, kilt
guinea	*k.i.t.ee.*	giddy, guinea
gum	*k.u.m.*	come, cup, gum, hub, hum
gums	*k.u.m.s.*	comes, cups, gums, hubs, hums
gun	*k.u.t.*	cut, cud, gun, gut, hut
guns	*k.u.t.s.*	cuts, guns, guts, huts
gurn	*k.er.t.*	curt, gird, gurn, heard, herd, hurt
gush	*k.u.j.*	gush, hush, hutch
gushed	*k.u.j.t.*	gushed, hushed, hutched

gut

gut	*k.u.t.*	cut, cud, gun, gut, hut
guts	*k.u.t.s.*	cuts, guns, guts, huts
gutting	*k.u.t.i.ng.*	cunning, cutting, gutting
gym	*j.i.m.*	chip, Jim, gym, ship
habit	*k.a.m.i.t.*	cabin, habit
hack	*k.a.k.*	hack, hark
had	*k.a.t.*	can, card, cart, cat, guard, had, hard, hat, heart
hadn't	*k.a.t.uu.t.t.*	can't, hadn't, hand
hail	*k.ay.l.*	hail, kale
hailed	*k.ay.l.t.*	hailed, *gales*
hair	*k.air.*	care, hair, hare
hairless	*k.air.l.e.s.*	careless, hairless
hake	*k.ay.k.*	cake, hake
half	*k.a.v.*	calf, half, have
hall	*k.aw.l.*	call, hall
halt	*k.aw.l.t.*	called, halt, hauled, *calls*
halves	*k.a.v.s.*	calves, halves, *carved*
ham	*k.a.m.*	cab, calm, cam, cap, carp, gap, ham, harm, harp
hammer	*k.a.m.er.*	hammer, harbour
hammered	*k.a.m.er.t.*	hammered, harboured
hand	*k.a.t.t.*	can't, hadn't, hand

handcuffed	*k.a.t.k.u.v.t.*	handcuffed, handcuffs
handcuffs	*k.a.t.k.u.v.s.*	handcuffed, handcuffs
handing	*k.a.t.t.i.ng.*	gardening, handing
handle	*k.a.t.t.l.*	candle, handle
handled	*k.a.t.t.l.t.*	candles, handles, *handled*
handles	*k.a.t.t.l.s.*	candles, handles, *handled*
hands	*k.a.t.s.*	cards, cats, guards, hands, harts, hats, hearts
hang	*k.a.ng.*	gang, hang
hanged	*k.a.ng.t.*	gangs, hanged
happens	*k.a.m.e.t.s.*	happens, garments
harbour	*k.a.m.er.*	hammer, harbour
harboured	*k.a.m.er.t.*	hammered, harboured
hard	*k.a.t.*	can, card, cart, cat, guard, had, hard, hat, heart
hardened	*k.a.t.e.t.t.*	garden, guarded, hardened, hearted
hardened	*k.a.t.e.t.t.*	gardened, hardened
hardens	*k.a.t.e.t.s.*	gardens, hardens
hare	*k.air.*	care, hair, hare
hark	*k.a.k.*	hack, hark

harm

harm	*k.a.m.*	cab, calm, cam, cap, carp, gap, ham, harm, harp
harp	*k.a.m.*	cab, calm, cam, cap, carp, gap, ham, harm, harp
harts	*k.a.t.s.*	cards, cats, guards, hands, harts, hats, hearts
has	*k.a.s.*	cars, gas, has
hash	*k.a.j.*	cadge, cash, hash, hatch
haste	*k.ay.s.t.*	gazed, haste
hat	*k.a.t.*	can, card, cart, cat, guard, had, hard, hat, heart
hatch	*k.a.j.*	cadge, cash, hash, hatch
hate	*k.ay.t.*	cane, gain, gait, gate, hate
hats	*k.a.t.s.*	cards, cats, guards, hands, harts, hats, hearts
hauled	*k.aw.l.t.*	called, halt, hauled, *calls*
hauling	*k.aw.l.i.ng.*	calling, hauling
have	*k.a.v.*	calf, half, have
having	*k.a.v.i.ng.*	carving, having
hay	*k.ay.*	gay, hay
haze	*k.ay.s.*	case, gaze, haze
he	*k.ee.*	he, key
head	*k.e.t.*	get, head

heading	*k.e.t.i.ng.*	getting, heading
heads	*k.e.t.s.*	gets, heads, hence
heal	*k.ee.l.*	heal, heel, keel
heap	*k.ee.m.*	heap, keep
heaped	*k.ee.m.t.*	heaped, *heaps, keeps*
heaping	*k.ee.m.i.ng.*	heaping, keeping
heaps	*k.ee.m.s.*	heaps, keeps, *heaped*
hear	*k.ear.*	gear, hear, here
heard	*k.er.t.*	curt, gird, gurn, heard, herd, hurt
heart	*k.a.t.*	can, card, cart, cat, guard, had, hard, hat, heart
hearted	*k.a.t.e.t.*	garden, guarded, hardened, hearted
hearts	*k.a.t.s.*	cards, cats, guards, hands, harts, hats, hearts
heat	*k.ee.t.*	heat, heed, keen, *geese, he's, keys*
hedge	*k.e.j.*	hedge, ketch
heed	*k.ee.t.*	heat, heed, keen, *geese, he's, keys*
heel	*k.ee.l.*	heal, heel, keel
height	*k.ii.t.*	guide, height, kite, *highs*
heightened	*k.ii.t.u.t.t.*	heightened, *kinds*
heights	*k.ii.t.s.*	heights, *hind, kind*

heir

heir	*air.*	air, heir
hemmed	*k.e.m.t.*	hemmed, kept
hence	*k.e.t.s.*	gets, heads, hence
herb	*k.er.m.*	curb, herb, *verb, blurb*
herbs	*k.er.m.s.*	curbs, herbs
herd	*k.er.t.*	curt, gird, gurn, heard, herd, hurt
herds	*k.er.t.s.*	herds, hurts
here	*k.ear.*	gear, hear, here
hers	*k.er.s.*	curse, hers
he's	*k.ee.s.*	geese, he's, keys, *heat, heed, keen, keyed*
hid	*k.i.t.*	hid, hit, kid, kit
hidden	*k.i.t.t.*	hidden, hint, *hits*
hide	*k.ii.t.*	guide, height, kite, *highs*
hiding	*k.ii.t.i.ng.*	guiding, hiding
highs	*k.ii.s.*	highs, *guide, height, hide, kite*
hill	*k.i.l.*	hill, kill, gill
hilled	*k.i.l.t.*	guild, guilt, hilled, hilt, killed, kiln, kilt
hills	*k.i.l.s.*	gills, hills, kills
hilt	*k.i.l.t.*	guild, guilt, hilled, hilt, killed, kiln, kilt
him	*k.i.m.*	him, hip, kip

hind	*k.ii.t.t.*	hind, kind, *heights*
hint	*k.i.t.t.*	hidden, hint, *hits*
hinted	*k.i.t.t.i.t.*	hinted, kindled
hip	*k.i.m.*	him, hip, kip
his	*k.i.s.*	his, kiss
hissed	*k.i.s.t.*	hissed, kissed
hissing	*k.i.s.i.ng.*	hissing,kissing
hit	*k.i.t.*	hid, hit, kid, kit
hits	*k.i.t.s.*	hits, *hidden, hint*
hoard	*k.aw.t.*	caught, chord, cord, corn, court, horn, hourd
hoarded	*k.aw.t.i.t.*	cornet, hoarded
hoarse	*k.aw.s.*	cause, coarse, course, horse
hod	*k.o.t.*	cod, cot, god, gone, got, hod, hot, *odd, on*
hods	*k.o.t.s.*	cots, gods, hods
hoe	*k.oh.*	hoe, go
hoeing	*k.oh.i.ng.*	going, hoeing, *owing*
hog	*k.o.k.*	hog, cock
hold	*k.oh.l.t.*	cold, gold, hold, holed
hole	*k.oh.l.*	coal, goal, hole, whole
holed	*k.oh.l.t.*	cold, gold, hold, holed
holes	*k.oh.l.s.*	coals, goals, holes

holy

holy	*k.oh.l.ee.*	coley, holy, wholly
home	*k.oh.m.*	home, hope, cope
homes	*k.oh.m.s.*	homes, hopes
honour	*o.t.er.*	honour, odder, otter, *hotter*
hood	*k.uu.t.*	could, good, hood
hook	*k.uu.k.*	cook, hook
hooked	*k.uu.k.t.*	cooked, hooked
hope	*k.oh.m.*	home, hope, cope
hopes	*k.oh.m.s.*	homes, hopes
hopper	*k.o.m.er.*	comma, copper, hopper
horn	*k.aw.t.*	caught, chord, cord, corn, court, horn, hourd
horse	*k.aw.s.*	cause, coarse, course, horse
host	*k.oh.s.t.*	coast, coaxed, ghost, host
hosting	*k.oh.s.t.i.ng.*	coasting, hosting
hot	*k.o.t.*	cod, cot, god, gone, got, hod, hot, *odd, on*
hotter	*k.o.t.er.*	hotter, *honour, odder, otter*
hound	*k.ow.t.t.*	count, gowned, hound
hour	*ow.er.*	hour, our, *cower*
house	*k.ow.s.*	cows, house
hovel	*k.o.v.u.l.*	hovel, *novel*

hover	k.o.v.er.	coffer, hover, *cover*
how	k.ow.	cow, how
hub	k.u.m.	come, cup, gum, hub, hum
hubs	k.u.m.s.	comes, cups, gums, hubs, hums
hum	k.u.m.	come, cup, gum, hub, hum
hums	k.u.m.s.	comes, cups, gums, hubs, hums
hurry	k.u.r.ee.	curry, hurry
hurt	k.er.t.	curt, gird, gurn, heard, herd, hurt
hurts	k.er.t.s.	herds, hurts
hush	k.u.j.	gush, hush, hutch
hushed	k.u.j.t.	gushed, hushed, hutched
hut	k.u.t.	cut, cud, gun, gut, hut
hutch	k.u.j.	gush, hush, hutch
hutched	k.u.j.t.	gushed, hushed, hutched
huts	k.u.t.s.	cuts, guns, guts, huts
ice	ii.s.	eyes, ice, *highs*
in	i.t.	in, inn, it
inch	i.t.j.	inch, *hinge*
indent	i.t.t.e.t.t.	indent, intend, intent
inn	i.t.	in, inn, it

inns

inns	*i.t.s.*	its, inns, *hits, hints*
intend	*i.t.t.e.t.t.*	indent, intend, intent
intent	*i.t.t.e.t.t.*	indent, intend, intent
it	*i.t.*	in, inn, it
its	*i.t.s.*	its, inns, *hits, hints*
jab	*j.a.m.*	chap, charm, jab, jam, sham, sharp
jack	*j.a.k.*	jack, shark
jam	*j.a.m.*	chap, charm, jab, jam, sham, sharp
jammed	*j.a.m.t.*	charmed, jammed
jape	*j.ay.m.*	jape, shame, shape
japed	*j.ay.m.t.*	japed, shamed, shaped
japes	*j.ay.m.s.*	japes, shames, shapes
jaw	*j.aw.*	chore, jaw, shore
jaws	*j.aw.s.*	chores, jaws, shores
jean	*j.ee.t.*	cheese, cheat, sheet, jean, sheet
jeans	*j.ee.t.s.*	jeans, sheets, cheats
jeer	*j.ee.r.*	cheer, jeer, shear, sheer
jet	*j.e.t.*	jet, shed
jets	*j.e.t.s.*	Jets, sheds
jim	*j.i.m.*	chip, Jim, gym, ship
job	*j.o.m.*	chop, job, shop

jobs	*j.o.m.s.*	chops, jobs
John	*J.o.t.*	John, jot, shod, shone, shot
joined	*j.oi.t.t.*	joined, joints, joint
joint	*j.oi.t.t.*	joined, joints, joint
joints	*j.oi.t.t.s.*	joined, joints, joint
joke	*j.oh.k.*	joke, choke
jokes	*j.oh.k.s.*	choked, chokes, jokes
jot	*j.o.t.*	John, jot, shod, shone, shot
juice	*j.oo.s.*	choose, juice, shoes
june	*j.oo.t.*	June, shoot
kale	*k.ay.l.*	hail, kale
keel	*k.ee.l.*	heal, heel, keel
keen	*k.ee.t.*	heat, heed, keen, *geese, he's, keys*
Keep	*K.ee.m.*	heap, keep
keeping	*k.ee.m.i.ng.*	heaping, keeping
keeps	*k.ee.m.s.*	heaps, keeps, *heaped*
kept	*k.e.m.t.*	hemmed, kept
ketch	*k.e.j.*	hedge, ketch
key	*k.ee.*	he, key
keys	*k.ee.s.*	geese, he's, keys, *heat, heed, keen, keyed*
kick	*k.i.k.*	gig, kick

kicks

kicks	k.i.k.s.	gigs, kicks
kid	k.i.t.	hid, hit, kid, kit
kill	k.i.l.	hill, kill, gill
killed	k.i.l.t.	guild, guilt, hilled, hilt, killed, kiln, kilt
kills	k.i.l.s.	gills, hills, kills
kiln	k.i.l.t.	guild, guilt, hilled, hilt, killed, kiln, kilt
kilt	k.i.l.t.	guild, guilt, hilled, hilt, killed, kiln, kilt
kind	k.ii.t.t.	hind, kind, *heights*
kindled	k.i.t.t.l.t.	hinted, kindled
kinds	k.ii.t.t.s.	kinds, *heightened*
kip	k.i.m.	him, hip, kip
kiss	k.i.s.	his, kiss
kissed	k.i.s.t.	hissed, kissed
kissing	k.i.s.i.ng.	hissing,kissing
kit	k.i.t.	hid, hit, kid, kit
kite	k.ii.t.	guide, height, kite, *highs*
knack	t.a.k.	knack, nag, tack, tag, *dank, tank*
knapped	t.a.m.t.	dabbed, dammed, damned,damped, knapped, nabbed, napped, tabbed, tamped, tapped
knee	t.ee.	knee, tea

kneel	*t.ee.l.*	deal, kneel
kneeler	*t.ee.l.er.*	dealer, kneeler
kneeling	*t.ee.l.i.ng.*	dealing, kneeling
knees	*t.ee.s.*	knees, niece, tease
knelt	*t.e.l.t.*	dealt, geld, knelt
knew	*t.ew.*	dew, due, knew, new
knife	*t.ii.v.*	dive, knife
knight	*t.ii.t.*	died, dine, dined, dyed, knight, night, nine, tide, tied, tight, tine
knighted	*t.ii.t.i.t.*	knighted, tidied
knights	*t.ii.t.s.*	dines, knights, nights, nines, tides, tights, tines
knit	*t.i.t.*	did, din, dint, knit, nit, tin, *didn't*
knives	*t.ii.v.s.*	dives, knives
knob	*t.o.m.*	dob, knob, nob, TOM, top
knobbed	*t.o.m.t.*	dobbed, knobbed, topped
knock	*t.o.k.*	dock, dog, knock, nog, tog
knocks	*t.o.k.s.*	docks, dogs, knocks, nogs, togs
knoll	*t.o.l.*	doll, knoll, toll

knot

knot	*t.o.t.*	don, dot, knot, nod, non, not, tot
knots	*t.o.t.s.*	dons, dots, knots, nods, tots
knotted	*t.o.t.e.t.*	knotted, nodded, totted
know	*t.oh.*	doe, dough, know, no, toe, tow, *toad, tone, towed*
knowing	*t.oh.i.ng.*	knowing, towing, *hoeing*
known	*t.oh.t.*	known, node, note, tone, tote
knows	*t.oh.s.*	doze, knows, nose, toes
lace	*l.ay.s.*	lace, laze, lays
lad	*l.a.t.*	lad, lard, *land*
ladder	*l.a.t.er.*	ladder, lander, latter
laid	*l.ay.t.*	laid, lane, late
lamb	*l.a.m.*	lamb, lap
land	*l.a.t.t.*	land, *lad, lard*
lander	*l.a.t.t.er.*	ladder, lander, latter
lane	*l.ay.t.*	laid, lane, late
lap	*l.a.m.*	lamb, lap
lard	*l.a.t.*	lad, lard, *land*
large	*l.a.j.*	large, latch
latch	*l.a.j.*	large, latch
late	*l.ay.t.*	laid, lane, late

latter	*l.a.t.er.*	ladder, lander, latter
lawn	*l.aw.t.*	lawn, lord
lawns	*l.aw.t.s.*	lawns, lords
lays	*l.ay.s.*	lace, laze, lays
laze	*l.ay.s.*	lace, laze, lays
leading	*l.ee.t.i.ng.*	leading, leaning
leaf	*l.ee.v.*	leaf, leave
league	*l.ee.k.*	leak, leek, league
leak	*l.ee.k.*	leak, leek, league
leaning	*l.ee.t.i.ng.*	leading, leaning
learned	*l.er.t.t.*	learned, learnt
learnt	*l.er.t.t.*	learned, learnt
leave	*l.ee.v.*	leaf, leave
led	*l.e.t.*	let, led
leek	*l.ee.k.*	leak, leek, league
lend	*l.e.t.t.*	lend, lent
lent	*l.e.t.t.*	lend, lent
let	*l.e.t.*	let, led
lice	*l.ii.s.*	lice, lies
lid	*l.i.t.*	lid, lit
lies	*l.ii.s.*	lice, lies
lift	*l.i.v.t.*	lift, lived
light	*l.ii.t.*	light, line

lighting

lighting	*l.ii.t.i.ng.*	lighting, lining
lights	*l.ii.t.s.*	lights, lines
limb	*l.i.m.*	limb, lip, *limp*
limbs	*l.i.m.s.*	limbs, lips
limp	*l.i.m.m.*	limp, *limb, lip*
line	*l.ii.t.*	light, line
lines	*l.ii.t.s.*	lights, lines
lining	*l.ii.t.i.ng.*	lighting, lining
lip	*l.i.m.*	limb, lip, *limp*
lips	*l.i.m.s.*	limbs, lips
list	*l.i.s.t.*	list, listen
listen	*l.i.s.t.*	list, listen
lit	*l.i.t.*	lid, lit
lived	*l.i.v.t.*	lift, lived
load	*l.oh.t.*	load, loan, lone
loan	*l.oh.t.*	load, loan, lone
lone	*l.oh.t.*	load, loan, lone
loose	*l.oo.s.*	loose, lose
loosing	*l.oo.s.i.ng.*	loosing, losing
Lord	*L.aw.t.*	lawn, lord
Lords	*L.aw.t.s.*	lawns, lords
lose	*l.oo.s.*	loose, lose
losing	*l.oo.s.i.ng.*	loosing, losing

lows	*l.oh.s.*	lows, *load, loan, lone*
luck	*l.u.k.*	luck, lug
lug	*l.u.k.*	luck, lug
mace	*m.ay.s.*	base, bass, mace, pace, pays
mad	*m.a.t.*	bad, ban, bard, barn, bat, mad, man, mat, pad, pan, part, pat
madder	*m.a.t.er.*	badder, banner, barter, batter, madder, manner, manor, matter, padder, patter
made	*m.ay.t.*	bade, bait, bane, made, maid, main, mane, mate, paid, pain, pane
maid	*m.ay.t.*	bade, bait, bane, made, maid, main, mane, mate, paid, pain, pane
maids	*m.ay.t.s.*	baits, banes, maids, mains, manes, mates, pains
mail	*m.ay.l.*	bail, mail, male, pail, pale
mails	*m.ay.l.s.*	bails, mails, males, pails
main	*m.ay.t.*	bade, bait, bane, made, maid, main, mane, mate, paid, pain, pane
mains	*m.ay.t.s.*	baits, banes, maids, mains, manes, mates, pains
make	*m.ay.k.*	bake, make

maker

maker	m.ay.k.er.	baker, maker
makers	m.ay.k.er.s.	bakers, makers
makes	m.ay.k.s.	bakes, makes
making	m.ay.k.i.ng.	baking, making
male	m.ay.l.	bail, mail, male, pail, pale
males	m.ay.l.s.	bails, mails, males, pails
mall	m.aw.l.	ball, mall, pall
malt	m.aw.l.t.	bald, malt, mauled
man	m.a.t.	bad, ban, bard, barn, bat, mad, man, mat, pad, pan, part, pat
mane	m.ay.t.	bade, bait, bane, made, maid, main, mane, mate, paid, pain, pane
maned	m.ay.t.t.	maned, pained, paint, paned
manes	m.ay.t.s.	baits, banes, maids, mains, manes, mates, pains
manly	m.a.t.l.ee.	badly, manly, partly
manned	m.a.t.t.	band, banned, manned, panned, pant, part
manner	m.a.t.er.	badder, banner, barter, batter, madder, manner, manor, matter, padder, patter
Manners	M.a.t.er.s.	banners, manners, matters, panders, patters

manor	*m.a.t.er.*	badder, banner, barter, batter, madder, manner, manor, matter, padder, patter
man's	*m.a.t.s.*	banns, barns, man's, pads, pans, pants, parts
mantel	*m.a.t.t.uu.l.*	battle, mantel, mantle, paddle, panel
mantle	*m.a.t.t.uu.l.*	battle, mantel, mantle, paddle, panel
many	*m.e.t.ee.*	many, penny, petty
map	*m.a.m.*	balm, map, palm
mapped	*m.a.m.t.*	balmed, barbed, mapped, palmed
maps	*m.a.m.s.*	balms, barbs, maps, palms
march	*m.a.j.*	badge, barge, batch, march, marsh, mash, match, patch
marches	*m.a.j.i.s.*	badges, barges, maches, marches, marshes, patches
mare	*m.air.*	bare, bear, mare, pair, pare, pear
mark	*m.a.k.*	back, bag, mark, pack, park
marked	*m.a.k.t.*	backed, bagged, barked, marked, packed, parked
marker	*m.a.k.er.*	backer, barker, marker, packer, parker

market

| market | *m.a.k.e.t.* | market, packet |
| marked | | |

market   *m.a.k.e.t.*   market, packet

markets   *m.a.k.e.t.s.*   markets, packets

marks   *m.a.k.s.*   backs, bags, barks, marks, parks

marred   *m.a.t.*   barred, marred

marriage   *m.a.r.i.j.*   bannish, marriage, parish

marrow   *m.a.r.oh.*   barrow, marrow

marrows   *m.a.r.oh.s.*   barrows, marrows

marsh   *m.a.j.*   badge, barge, batch, march, marsh, mash, match, patch

marshes   *m.a.j.i.s.*   badges, barges, maches, marches, marshes, patches

mash   *m.a.j.*   badge, barge, batch, march, marsh, mash, match, patch

masher   *m.a.j.er.*   badger, masher

massive   *m.a.s.i.v.*   massive, passive

mast   *m.a.s.t.*   mast, passed, past

mat   *m.a.t.*   bad, ban, bard, barn, bat, mad, man, mat, pad, pan, part, pat

match   *m.a.j.*   badge, barge, batch, march, marsh, mash, match, patch

matches	*m.a.j.e.s.*	badges, barges, maches, marches, marshes, patches
mate	*m.ay.t.*	bade, bait, bane, made, maid, main, mane, mate, paid, pain, pane
mates	*m.ay.t.s.*	baits, banes, maids, mains, manes, mates, pains
mats	*m.a.t.s.*	banns, barns, man's, pads, pans, pants, parts
matted	*m.a.t.i.t.*	batted, matted, parted, patted
matter	*m.a.t.er.*	badder, banner, barter, batter, madder, manner, manor, matter, padder, patter
mattered	*m.a.t.er.t.*	bantered, battered, mattered, pattern, patterned
matters	*m.a.t.er.s.*	banners, manners, matters, panders, patters
mauled	*m.aw.l.t.*	bald, malt, mauled
may	*m.ay.*	bay, may, pay
maybe	*m.ay.m.ee.*	baby, maybe
mazes	*m.ay.s.i.s.*	bases, basis, mazes, paces
me	*m.ee.*	be, bee, me, pea
meal	*m.ee.l.*	meel, peal, peel

meals

meals	*m.ee.l.s.*	meals, peals, peels
mean	*m.ee.t.*	bean, beat, been, beet, mean, meat, meet, peat
meaning	*m.ee.t.i.ng.*	beating, meaning, meeting
means	*m.ee.t.s.*	beads, beans, beats, beets, means, meats, meets, peats
meant	*m.e.t.t.*	bend, bent, bet, men, meant, mend, met, pen, penned, pent, pet
measles	*m.ee.s.l.s.*	measles, pieces
meat	*m.ee.t.*	bean, beat, been, beet, mean, meat, meet, peat
meats	*m.ee.t.s.*	beads, beans, beats, beets, means, meats, meets, peats
medal	*m.e.t.l.*	medal, metal, pedal, petal
medals	*m.e.t.u.l.s.*	medals, metals, pedals, petals
meet	*m.ee.t.*	bean, beat, been, beet, mean, meat, meet, peat
meeting	*m.ee.t.i.ng.*	beating, meaning, meeting
meets	*m.ee.t.s.*	beads, beans, beats, beets, means, meats, meets, peats
melt	*m.e.l.t.*	belt, melt, pelt

men	*m.e.t.*	bed, bet, men, met, pen, pet
men	*m.e.t.*	bend, bent, bet, men, meant, mend, met, pen, penned, pent, pet
mend	*m.e.t.t.*	bend, bent, bet, men, meant, mend, met, pen, penned, pent, pet
men's	*t.e.t.s.*	beds, bets, men's, pence, pens, pets
mention	*m.e.t.j.u.t.*	mention, mentioned
mentioned	*m.e.t.j.u.t.t.*	mention, mentioned
mercy	*m.er.s.ee.*	mercy, MERSEY, PERCY
mere	*m.ear.*	beer, bier, mere, peer, pier
merit	*m.e.r.i.t.*	buried, merit
merry	*m.e.r.ee.*	berry, merry, perry
MERSEY	*M.ER.S.EE.*	mercy, MERSEY, PERCY
messed	*m.e.s.t.*	best, messed, pest
met	*m.e.t.*	bed, bet, men, met, pen, pet
met	*m.e.t.*	bend, bent, bet, men, meant, mend, met, pen, penned, pent, pet
metal	*m.e.t.u.l.*	medal, metal, pedal, petal

metals

metals	*m.e.t.uu.l.s.*	medals, metals, pedals, petals
meter	*m.ee.t.er.*	beader, beater, meter, metre, PETER
metre	*m.ee.t.er.*	beader, beater, meter, metre, PETER
mew	*m.ew.*	mew, pew
mews	*m.ew.s.*	mews, pews
MICK	*M.I.K.*	big, MICK, pick, pig
mid	*m.i.t.*	bid, bin, bit, mid, pin, pit
might	*m.ii.t.*	bide, bind, bite, might, mind, mine, mite, pied
MIKE	*M.II.K.*	bike, MIKE, pike
mile	*m.ii.l.*	bile, mile, pile
miles	*m.ii.l.s.*	biles, miles, piles
mill	*m.i.l.*	bill, mill, pill
milled	*m.i.l.t.*	billed, build, built, milled, milt
million	*m.i.l.ee.u.t.*	billion, million, pillion
millions	*m.i.l.ee.u.t.s.*	billions, millions
mills	*m.i.l.s.*	bills, mills, pills
milt	*m.i.l.t.*	billed, build, built, milled, milt
mince	*m.i.t.s.*	bids, bins, bits, mince, pins, pits

mind

mind	*m.ii.t.t.*	bide, bind, bite, might, mind, mine, mite, pied
minding	*m.ii.t.t.i.ng.*	binding, biting, mining,minding
minds	*m.ii.t.t.s.*	binds, bites, minds, mites, pints
mine	*m.ii.t.*	bide, bind, bite, might, mind, mine, mite, pied
miner	*m.ii.t.er.*	miner, mitre, myna
mini	*m.i.t.ee.*	mini, pinny, pity
mining	*m.ii.t.i.ng.*	binding, biting, mining,minding
minted	*m.i.t.t.i.t.*	minted, minute, pitied
minute	*m.i.t.i.t.*	minted, minute, pitied
mirth	*m.er.th.*	birth, mirth, PERTH
miss	*m.i.s.*	miss, mix, piss
missed	*m.i.s.t.*	missed, mist, mixed,
misses	*m.i.s.i.s.*	misses, Mrs
mist	*m.i.s.t.*	missed, mist, mixed,
mite	*m.ii.t.*	bide, bind, bite, might, mind, mine, mite, pied
mites	*m.ii.t.s.*	binds, bites, minds, mites, pints
mitre	*m.ii.t.er.*	miner, mitre, myna
mix	*m.i.s.*	miss, mix, piss
mixed	*m.i.s.t.*	missed, mist, mixed,

moan

moan	*m.oh.t.*	boat, bode, bone, moan, moat, mode, mowed
moan	*m.oh.t.*	boat, bone, moan
moaned	*m.oh.t.t.*	boned, moaned
moaning	*m.oh.t.i.ng.*	boating, moaning
moans	*m.oh.t.s.*	boats, bones, moans
moat	*m.oh.t.*	boat, bode, bone, moan, moat, mode, mowed
mob	*m.o.m.*	bob, bomb, mob, mop, pop, *pomp*
mobbing	*m.o.m.i.ng.*	bobbing, bombing, mobbing, mopping, popping
mode	*m.oh.t.*	boat, bode, bone, moan, moat, mode, mowed
model	*m.o.t.l.*	bottle, model, mottle
models	*m.o.t.uu.l.s.*	bottles, models, mottles
mole	*m.oh.l.*	bowl, mole, pole
moles	*m.oh.l.s.*	bowls, moles, poles
money	*m.u.t.ee.*	bunny, money, muddy, putty
mood	*m.oo.t.*	booed, boon, boot, mood, moon, moot
mood	*m.oo.t.*	boon, boot, mood, moon, moot
moods	*m.oo.t.s.*	boons, boots, moods, moons, moots

moon	*m.oo.t.*	booed, boon, boot, mood, moon, moot
moon	*m.oo.t.*	boon, boot, mood, moon, moot
moons	*m.oo.t.s.*	boons, boots, moods, moons, moots
moor	*m.aw.*	bore, moor, more, poor, pore
moored	*m.aw.t.*	board, bored, born, bourne, bought, moored, pawned, poured, port
mooring	*m.oo.r.i.ng.*	boring, mooring, pouring
moot	*m.oo.t.*	booed, boon, boot, mood, moon, moot
moot	*m.oo.t.*	boon, boot, mood, moon, moot
mooted	*m.oo.t.i.t.*	booted, mooted
moots	*m.oo.t.s.*	boons, boots, moods, moons, moots
mop	*m.o.m.*	bob, bomb, mob, mop, pop, *pomp*
mopping	*m.o.m.i.ng.*	bobbing, bombing, mobbing, mopping, popping
more	*m.aw.*	bore, moor, more, poor, pore
morning	*m.aw.t.i.ng.*	boarding, morning, mourning, pawning
morrow	*m.o.r.oh.*	borrow, morrow

mortal

mortal	*m.aw.t.l.*	mortal, portal
mortar	*m.aw.t.er.*	boarder, border, mortar, mourner, pawner, porter
moss	*m.o.s.*	boss, box, moss, pox
mossed	*m.o.s.t.*	bossed, boxed, mossed, poxed
mosses	*m.o.s.i.s.*	bosses, boxes, mosses, poxes
most	*m.oh.s.t.*	boast, most, post
motor	*m.oh.t.er.*	boater, motor
motors	*m.oh.t.er.s.*	boaters, motors
mottle	*m.o.t.uu.l.*	bottle, model, mottle
mottles	*m.o.ttl.s.*	bottles, models, mottles
mould	*m.oh.l.t.*	bold, bolt, mould, moult, poult
moulded	*m.oh.l.t.i.t.*	bolted, moulded
moulding	*m.oh.l.t.i.ng.*	bolting, moulding, balding
moult	*m.oh.l.t.*	bold, bolt, mould, moult, poult
mound	*m.ow.t.t.*	bound, mound, mount, pound
mounds	*m.ow.t.t.s.*	bounds, mounts, pounds, *bounce, pounce*
mount	*m.ow.t.t.*	bound, mound, mount, pound

mounted	m.ow.t.t.e.t.	mounted, pounded, *pouted*
mounting	m.ow.t.t.i.ng.	mounting, pounding
mounts	m.ow.t.t.s.	bounds, mounts, pounds, *bounce, pounce*
mourner	m.aw.t.er.	boarder, border, mortar, mourner, pawner, porter
mourning	m.aw.t.i.ng.	boarding, morning, mourning, pawning
mowed	m.oh.t.	boat, bode, bone, moan, moat, mode, mowed
Mrs	M.i.s.i.s.	misses, Mrs
much	m.u.j.	budge, mush, much
muck	m.u.k.	buck, bug, muck, mug, pug
mud	m.u.t.	bud, bun, but, butt, mud, pun, putt
mud	m.u.t.	bud, bun, but, butt, mud, pun, putt
muddle	m.u.t.l.	muddle, puddle
muddy	m.u.t.ee.	bunny, money, muddy, putty
muffed	m.u.v.t.	buffed, muffed, puffed
muffin	m.u.v.i.t.	muffin, puffin
mug	m.u.k.	buck, bug, muck, mug, pug

mum

mum	*m.u.m.*	bum, mum, pub, pup, *bump, pump*
mumps	*m.u.m.m.s.*	bumps, mumps, pumps, *bums, mums, pubs, pups*
munch	*m.u.t.j.*	bunch, munch, punch
murky	*m.er.k.ee.*	murky, perky
muscle	*m.u.s.uu.l.*	bustle, muscle, muzzle, puzzle
muscled	*m.u.s.uu.l.t.*	bustled, muscled, muzzled, puzzled
muscles	*m.u.s.l.s.*	bustles, muscles, muzzles, puzzles
mush	*m.u.j.*	budge, mush, much
must	*m.u.s.t.*	bussed, bust, must
mutter	*m.u.t.er.*	butter, mutter, putter
muttered	*m.u.t.er.t.*	buttered, muttered
mutton	*m.u.t.o.t.*	button, mutton
mutton	*m.u.t.o.t.*	button, mutton
muzzle	*m.u.s.l.*	bustle, muscle, muzzle, puzzle
muzzled	*m.u.s.l.t.*	bustled, muscled, muzzled, puzzled
muzzles	*m.u.zzuu.l.s.*	bustles, muscles, muzzles, puzzles
my	*m.ii.*	buy, by, bye, my, pie
myna	*m.ii.t.er.*	miner, mitre, myna

nab	*t.a.m.*	dab, dam, damn, damp, nab, nap, tab, tamp, tap
nabbed	*t.a.m.t.*	dabbed, dammed, damned,damped, knapped, nabbed, napped, tabbed, tamped, tapped
nabbing	*t.a.m.i.ng.*	dabbing, damming, nabbing, napping, tabbing, tamping, tapping, *napkin*
nabs	*t.a.m.s.*	dabs, dams, nabs, naps, tabs, tamps, taps
nag	*t.a.k.*	knack, nag, tack, tag, *dank, tank*
nags	*t.a.k.s.*	nags, tags, tax
nail	*t.ay.l.*	dale, nail, tail, tale, *snail, stale*
nails	*t.ay.l.s.*	dales, nails, tails, tales, *snails*
name	*t.ay.m.*	dame, name, nape, tame, tape
named	*t.ay.m.t.*	named, tamed, taped
namer	*t.ay.m.er.*	neighbour, namer, tamer, taper
names	*t.ay.m.s.*	dames, names, napes, tames, tapes
naming	*t.ay.m.i.ng.*	naming, taming, taping

nap

nap	*t.a.m.*	dab, dam, damn, damp, nab, nap, tab, tamp, tap
nape	*t.ay.m.*	dame, name, nape, tame, tape
napes	*t.ay.m.s.*	dames, names, napes, tames, tapes
napkin	*t.a.m.k.i.t.*	napkin, *damming, nabbing, napping, tabbing, tamping, tapping*
napped	*t.a.m.t.*	dabbed, dammed, damned,damped, knapped, nabbed, napped, tabbed, tamped, tapped
napping	*t.a.m.i.ng.*	dabbing, damming, nabbing, napping, tabbing, tamping, tapping, *napkin*
naps	*t.a.m.s.*	dabs, dams, nabs, naps, tabs, tamps, taps
nark	*t.a.k.*	dark, nark
native	*t.ay.t.i.v.*	dative, native
natters	*t.a.t.er.s.*	natters, tanners, tatters
natty	*t.a.t.ee.*	daddy, dandy, natty, tatty, *darted, tarded, tanzy*
neap	*t.ee.m.*	deem, deep, neap, team
near	*t.ear.*	dear, deer, near, tear
near	*t.ear.*	dear, near, tear

nearer	*t.ear.r.er.*	dearer, nearer
nearest	*t.ear.r.e.s.t.*	dearest, nearest
neat	*t.ee.t.*	dean, deed, neat, need, teat, teen
neck	*t.e.k.*	deck, neck
need	*t.ee.t.*	dean, deed, neat, need, teat, teen
needs	*t.ee.t.s.*	deans, deeds, needs, teats, teens
neigh	*t.ay.*	day, neigh, TAY
neighbour	*t.ay.m.er.*	neighbour, namer, tamer, taper
nerd	*t.er.t.*	dirt, nerd, turd, turn
nest	*t.e.s.t.*	nest, next, test, text
net	*t.e.t.*	dead, debt, den, net, ten, *dent,tent*
never	*t.e.v.er.*	never, *tether*
new	*t.ew.*	dew, due, knew, new
newly	*t.ew.l.ee.*	duly, newly
news	*t.ew.s.*	deuce, news, *newts*
newt	*t.ew.t.*	nude, newt, tune, *dune*
newts	*t.ew.t.s.*	newts, *deuce, news*
next	*t.e.s.t.*	nest, next, test, text
nib	*t.i.m.*	dib, dim, dip, nib, nip, TIM, tip

nibbed

nibbed	*t.i.m.t.*	dibbed, dimmed, dipped, nibbed, nipped, tipped,
nibs	*t.i.m.s.*	dips, dims, dips, nibs, nips, tips
nice	*t.ii.s.*	dice, dyes, nice, ties
niche	*t.ee.j.*	dish, ditch, niche, titch
nick	*t.i.k.*	DICK, dig, nick, tick, tig
nick it	*t.i.k. i.t.*	dig it, nick it, ticket
nicked	*t.i.k.t.*	nicked, ticked
nicker	*t.i.k.er.*	dicker, nicker, nigger, ticker
nicking	*t.i.k.i.ng.*	digging, nicking, ticking
nicks	*t.i.k.s.*	digs, nicks, ticks
niece	*t.ee.s.*	knees, niece, tease
nigger	*t.i.k.er.*	dicker, nicker, nigger, ticker
niggled	*t.i.k.uu.l.t.*	niggled, tickled
nigh	*t.ii.*	die, nigh, tie
night	*t.ii.t.*	died, dine, dined, dyed, knight, night, nine, tide, tied, tight, tine
nightly	*t.ii.t.l.ee.*	nightly, tightly
nights	*t.ii.t.s.*	dines, knights, nights, nines, tides, tights, tines
nil	*t.i.l.*	dill, nil, till

nimble	*t.i.m.m.l.*	dimple, nimble, nipple, tipple
nimbly	*t.i.m.m.l.ee.*	nimbly, *dimly*
nine	*t.ii.t.*	died, dine, dined, dyed, knight, night, nine, tide, tied, tight, tine
nines	*t.ii.t.s.*	dines, knights, nights, nines, tides, tights, tines
nineteen	*t.ii.t.t.ee.t.*	ninteen, *ninety*
ninety	*t.ii.t.t.ee.*	ninety, *nineteen*
nip	*t.i.m.*	dib, dim, dip, nib, nip, TIM, tip
nipped	*t.i.m.t.*	dibbed, dimmed, dipped, nibbed, nipped, tipped,
nipper	*t.i.m.er.*	dibber, dimmer, dipper, nipper, timber, tipper
nipple	*t.i.m.uu.l.*	dimple, nimble, nipple, tipple
nipples	*t.i.m.uu.l.s.*	dimples, nipples, tipples
nips	*t.i.m.s.*	dips, dims, dips, nibs, nips, tips
nit	*t.i.t.*	did, din, dint, knit, nit, tin, *didn't*
no	*t.oh.*	doe, dough, know, no, toe, tow, *toad, tone, towed*
nob	*t.o.m.*	dob, knob, nob, TOM, top

nod

nod	*t.o.t.*	don, dot, knot, nod, non, not, tot
nodded	*t.o.t.e.t.*	knotted, nodded, totted
node	*t.oh.t.*	known, node, note, tone, tote
nodes	*t.oh.t.s.*	dotes, nodes, notes, toads, tones
nods	*t.o.t.s.*	dons, dots, knots, nods, tots
nog	*t.o.k.*	dock, dog, knock, nog, tog
nogs	*t.o.k.s.*	docks, dogs, knocks, nogs, togs
noise	*t.oi.s.*	noise, toys
non	*t.o.t.*	don, dot, knot, nod, non, not, tot
none	*t.u.t.*	done, dud, none, nut, tonne, ton
nook	*t.oo.k.*	nook, took
nor	*t.aw.*	door, gnaw, nor, tore, tour
nose	*t.oh.s.*	doze, knows, nose, toes
noses	*t.oh.s.i.s.*	dozes, noses
not	*t.o.t.*	don, dot, knot, nod, non, not, tot
notched	*t.o.j.t.*	dodged, notched

note	*t.oh.t.*	known, node, note, tone, tote
noted	*t.oh.t.i.t.*	doted, noted
notes	*t.oh.t.s.*	dotes, nodes, notes, toads, tones
nought	*t.aw.t.*	dawn, gnawed, nought, torn, tort, toured, taught
noun	*t.ow.t.*	doubt, down, noun, nowt, town
nouns	*t.ow.t.s.*	doubts, downs, nouns,toutes, towns
novel	*t.o.v.e.l.*	novel, *hovel*
now	*t.ow.*	dhow, now
nowt	*t.ow.t.*	doubt, down, noun, nowt, town
nude	*t.ew.t.*	nude, newt, tune, *dune*
null	*t.u.l.*	dull, null
numb	*t.u.m.t.*	dumb, numb, tub, *dump*
numbed	*t.u.m.t.*	dumbed, numbed
number	*t.u.m.m.er.*	dumper, number
numbers	*t.u.m.m.er.s.*	dumpers, numbers
nun	*t.u.t.*	done, dud, none, nut, tonne, ton
nuns	*t.u.t.s.*	duds, nuns, nuts, tonnes, tons
nurse	*t.er.s.*	nurse, terse

nut

nut	*t.u.t.*	done, dud, none, nut, tonne, ton
nuts	*t.u.t.s.*	duds, nuns, nuts, tonnes, tons
oar	*aw.*	awe, oar, or
oars	*aw.s.*	oars, horse
ocher	*oh.k.er.*	ochre/ocher, ogre
ochre	*oh.k.er.*	ochre/ocher, ogre
odd	*o.t.*	odd, on, *cod, cot, god, gone, got, hod, hot*
odder	*o.t.er.*	honour, odder, otter, *hotter*
of	*o.v.*	of, off
off	*o.v.*	of, off
offence	*o.v.e.t.s.*	offence, offends
offender	*o.v.e.t.t.er.*	offender, oftener
offends	*u.v.e.t.t.s.*	offence, offends
offered	*o.v.er.t.*	offered, overt
oftener	*o.v.e.t.t.er.*	offender, oftener
ogre	*oh.k.er.*	ochre/ocher, ogre
oil	*oi.l.*	oil, *coil*
oiled	*oi.l.t.*	oiled, *coiled*
on	*o.t.*	odd, on, *cod, cot, god, gone, got, hod, hot*
Once	*W.u.t.s.*	once, ones

one	*w.u.t.*	one, won
ones	*w.u.t.s.*	once, ones
or	*aw.*	awe, oar, or
order	*aw.t.er.*	order, corder, corner
ordered	*aw.t.er.t.*	ordered, cornered
ordering	*aw.t.er.i.ng.*	ordering, cornering
orders	*aw.t.er.s.*	orders, corders, corners
otter	*o.t.er.*	honour, odder, otter, *hotter*
ought	*aw.t.*	aught, awed, awn, ought
our	*ow.er.*	hour, our, *cower*
Ours	*OW.er.s.*	ours, *cowers*
out	*ow.t.*	out, *gown, gout*
overt	*oh.v.er.t.*	offered, overt
owe	*oh.w.*	owe, *go, hoe*
owed	*oh.t.*	owed, own
owing	*oh.i.ng.*	owing, *going, hoeing*
owl	*ow.l.*	owl, *cowl*
own	*oh.t.*	owed, own
pace	*m.ay.s.*	base, bass, mace, pace, pays
paces	*m.ay.s.e.s.*	bases, basis, mazes, paces

pack

pack	*m.a.k.*	back, bag, mark, pack, park
packed	*m.a.k.t.*	backed, bagged, barked, marked, packed, parked
packer	*m.a.k.er.*	backer, barker, marker, packer, parker
packet	*m.a.k.i.t.*	market, packet
packets	*m.a.k.e.t.s.*	markets, packets
packing	*m.a.k.i.ng.*	backing, packing
pad	*m.a.t.*	bad, ban, bard, barn, bat, mad, man, mat, pad, pan, part, pat
padder	*m.a.t.er.*	badder, banner, barter, batter, madder, manner, manor, matter, padder, patter
paddle	*m.a.t.l.*	battle, mantel, mantle, paddle, panel
pads	*m.a.t.s.*	banns, barns, man's, pads, pans, pants, parts
page	*m.ay.j.*	beige, page
paid	*m.ay.t.*	bade, bait, bane, made, maid, main, mane, mate, paid, pain, pane
pail	*m.ay.l.*	bail, mail, male, pail, pale
pails	*payl.s.*	bails, mails, males, pails
pain	*m.ay.t.*	bade, bait, bane, made, maid, main, mane, mate, paid, pain, pane

pained	*m.ay.t.t.*	maned, pained, paint, paned
pains	*m.ay.t.s.*	baits, banes, maids, mains, manes, mates, pains
paint	*m.ay.t.t.*	maned, pained, paint, paned
pair	*m.air.*	bare, bear, mare, pair, pare, pear
pale	*m.ay.l.*	bail, mail, male, pail, pale
pall	*m.aw.l.*	ball, mall, pall
palm	*m.a.m.*	balm, map, palm
palmed	*m.a.m.t.*	balmed, barbed, mapped, palmed
palms	*m.a.m.s.*	balms, barbs, maps, palms
pan	*m.a.t.*	bad, ban, bard, barn, bat, mad, man, mat, pad, pan, part, pat
panders	*m.a.t.t.er.s.*	banners, manners, matters, panders, patters
pane	*m.ay.t.*	bade, bait, bane, made, maid, main, mane, mate, paid, pain, pane
paned	*m.ay.t.t.*	maned, pained, paint, paned
panel	*m.a.t.e.l.*	battle, mantel, mantle, paddle, panel

panned

panned	*m.a.t.t.*	band, banned, manned, panned, pant, part
pans	*m.a.t.s.*	banns, barns, man's, pads, pans, pants, parts
pant	*m.a.t.t.*	band, banned, manned, panned, pant, part
pants	*m.a.t.t.s.*	banns, barns, man's, pads, pans, pants, parts
pare	*m.alr.*	bare, bear, mare, pair, pare, pear
paring	*m.air.i.ng.*	baring, bearing, paring
parish	*m.a.r.i.j.*	bannish, marriage, parish
park	*m.a.k.*	back, bag, mark, pack, park
parked	*m.a.k.t.*	backed, bagged, barked, marked, packed, parked
parker	*m.a.k.er.*	backer, barker, marker, packer, parker
parks	*m.a.k.s.*	backs, bags, barks, marks, parks
part	*m.a.t.*	bad, ban, bard, barn, bat, mad, man, mat, pad, pan, part, pat
part	*m.a.t.*	band, banned, manned, panned, pant, part
parted	*m.a.t.e.t.*	batted, matted, parted, patted
partly	*m.a.t.l.ee.*	badly, manly, partly

parts	*m.a.t.s.*	banns, barns, man's, pads, pans, pants, parts
pass	*m.a.s.*	bars, pass
passed	*m.a.s.t.*	mast, passed, past
passive	*m.a.s.i.v.*	massive, passive
past	*m.a.s.t.*	mast, passed, past
paste	*m.ay.s.t.*	based, paste
pat	*m.a.t.*	bad, ban, bard, barn, bat, mad, man, mat, pad, pan, part, pat
patch	*m.a.j.*	badge, barge, batch, march, marsh, mash, match, patch
patches	*m.a.j.e.s.*	badges, barges, maches, marches, marshes, patches
path	*m.a.th.*	bath, path
patted	*m.a.t.e.t.*	batted, matted, parted, patted
patter	*m.a.t.er.*	badder, banner, barter, batter, madder, manner, manor, matter, padder, patter
pattern	*m.a.t.er.t.*	bantered, battered, mattered, pattern, patterned
patterned	*m.a.t.er.t.t.*	bantered, battered, mattered, pattern, patterned

patters

patters	*m.a.t.er.s.*	banners, manners, matters, panders, patters
pawned	*m.aw.t.t.*	board, bored, born, bourne, bought, moored, pawned, poured, port
pawner	*m.aw.t.er.*	boarder, border, mortar, mourner, pawner, porter
pawning	*m.aw.t.i.ng.*	boarding, morning, mourning, pawning
pay	*m.ay.*	bay, may, pay
paying	*m.ay.i.ng.*	baying, paying
pays	*m.ay.s.*	base, bass, mace, pace, pays
pea	*m.ee.*	be, bee, me, pea
peace	*m.ee.s.*	bees, peace, peas, piece
peach	*m.ee.j.*	beach, peach
peal	*m.ee.l.*	meel, peal, peel
peals	*m.ee.l.s.*	meals, peals, peels
pear	*m.air.*	bare, bear, mare, pair, pare, pear
peas	*m.ee.s.*	bees, peace, peas, piece
peat	*m.ee.t.*	bean, beat, been, beet, mean, meat, meet, peat
peats	*m.ee.t.s.*	beads, beans, beats, beets, means, meats, meets, peats
peck	*m.e.k.*	beck, beg, peck, peg

pecking	*m.e.k.i.ng.*	begging, pegging, pecking
pedal	*m.e.t.u.l.*	medal, metal, pedal, petal
pedals	*m.e.t.u.l.s.*	medals, metals, pedals, petals
peel	*m.ee.l.*	meel, peal, peel
peels	*m.ee.l.s.*	meals, peals, peels
peeped	*m.ee.m.t.*	beamed, peeped
peer	*m.ear.*	beer, bier, mere, peer, pier
peg	*m.e.k.*	beck, beg, peck, peg
pegging	*m.e.k.i.ng.*	begging, pegging, pecking
pelt	*m.e.l.t.*	belt, melt, pelt
pen	*m.e.t.*	bed, bet, men, met, pen, pet
pen	*m.e.t.*	bend, bent, bet, men, meant, mend, met, pen, penned, pent, pet
pence	*m.e.t.s.*	beds, bets, men's, pence, pens, pets
penned	*m.e.t.t.*	bend, bent, bet, men, meant, mend, met, pen, penned, pent, pet
penny	*m.e.t.ee.*	many, penny, petty
pens	*m.e.t.s.*	beds, bets, men's, pence, pens, pets

pent

pent	*m.e.t.t.*	bend, bent, bet, men, meant, mend, met, pen, penned, pent, pet
perch	*m.er.j.*	birch, perch
PERCY	*M.ER.S.EE.*	mercy, MERSEY, PERCY
perky	*m.er.k.ee.*	murky, perky
perry	*m.e.r.ee.*	berry, merry, perry
person	*m.er.s.o.t.*	burst, person
pert	*m.er.t.*	bird, BERT, burn, pert
PERTH	*M.ER.TH.*	birth, mirth, PERTH
pest	*m.e.s.t.*	best, messed, pest
pet	*m.e.t.*	bed, bet, men, met, pen, pet
pet	*m.e.t.*	bend, bent, bet, men, meant, mend, met, pen, penned, pent, pet
petal	*m.e.t.uu.l.*	medal, metal, pedal, petal
petals	*m.e.t.uu.l.s.*	medals, metals, pedals, petals
PETER	*M.EE.T.ER.*	beader, beater, meter, metre, PETER
pets	*m.e.t.s.*	beds, bets, men's, pence, pens, pets
petty	*m.e.t.ee.*	many, penny, petty
pew	*m.ew.*	mew, pew
pews	*m.ew.s.*	mews, pews

phone	*v.oh.t.*	phone, vote
phoning	*v.oh.t.i.ng.*	phoning, voting
pick	*m.i.k.*	big, MICK, pick, pig
pie	*m.ii.*	buy, by, bye, my, pie
piece	*m.ee.s.*	bees, peace, peas, piece
pieced	*m.ee.s.t.*	beast, pieced
pieces	*m.ee.s.i.s.*	measles, pieces
pied	*m.ii.t.*	bide, bind, bite, might, mind, mine, mite, pied
pier	*m.ear.*	beer, bier, mere, peer, pier
pig	*m.i.k.*	big, MICK, pick, pig
pike	*m.ii.k.*	bike, MIKE, pike
pile	*m.ii.l.*	bile, mile, pile
piles	*m.ii.l.s.*	biles, miles, piles
pill	*m.i.l.*	bill, mill, pill
pillion	*m.i.l.ee.u.t.*	billion, million, pillion
pills	*m.i.l.s.*	bills, mills, pills
pin	*m.i.t.*	bid, bin, bit, mid, pin, pit
pinny	*m.i.t.ee.*	mini, pinny, pity
pins	*m.i.t.s.*	bids, bins, bits, mince, pins, pits
pints	*m.ii.t.t.s.*	binds, bites, minds, mites, pints

pip

pip	*m.i.m.*	bib, pip
pips	*m.i.m.s.*	bibs, pips
piss	*m.i.s.*	miss, mix, piss
pit	*m.i.t.*	bid, bin, bit, mid, pin, pit
pitch	*m.i.j.*	bitch, pitch
pitied	*m.i.t.i.t.*	minted, minute, pitied
pits	*m.i.t.s.*	bids, bins, bits, mince, pins, pits
pity	*m.i.t.ee.*	mini, pinny, pity
place	*m.l.ay.s.*	blaze, place, plays
placing	*m.l.ay.s.i.ng.*	blazing, placing
plain	*m.l.ay.t.*	blade, plain, plane, plate, played
plains	*m.l.ay.t.s.*	blades, plains, plates
plait	*m.l.ay.t.*	plan, plait, *plant, planned*
plan	*m.l.a.t.*	plan, plait, *plant, planned*
plane	*m.l.ay.t.*	blade, plain, plane, plate, played
plank	*m.l.a.ng.k.*	blank, plank
plant	*m.l.a.t.t.*	plant, *planned, plan, plait*
plate	*m.l.ay.t.*	blade, plain, plane, plate, played
plates	*m.l.ay.t.s.*	blades, plains, plates

played	*m.l.ay.t.*	blade, plain, plane, plate, played
plays	*m.l.ay.s.*	blaze, place, plays
pleaded	*m.l.ee.t.i.t.*	bleated, pleaded, pleated
pleading	*m.l.ee.t.i.ng.*	bleeding, bleating, pleading, pleating
pleated	*m.l.ee.t.i.t.*	bleated, pleaded, pleated
pleating	*m.l.ee.t.i.ng.*	bleeding, bleating, pleading, pleating
plight	*m.l.ii.t.*	blight, plight
plighted	*m.l.ii.t.i.t.*	blighted, plighted
plod	*m.l.o.t.*	blot, pled, plot
plodders	*m.l.o.t.er.s.*	blotters, plodders, plotters
plodding	*m.l.o.t.i.ng.*	blotting, plodding, plotting
plods	*m.l.o.t.s.*	blots, plods, plots
plot	*m.l.o.t.*	blot, pled, plot
plots	*m.l.o.t.s.*	blots, plods, plots
plotters	*m.l.o.t.er.s.*	blotters, plodders, plotters
plotting	*m.l.o.t.i.ng.*	blotting, plodding, plotting
pluck	*m.l.u.k.*	pluck, plug
plucked	*m.l.u.k.t.*	plucked, plugged

plucking

plucking	*m.l.u.k.i.ng.*	plucking, plugging
plug	*m.l.u.k.*	pluck, plug
plugged	*m.l.u.k.t.*	plucked, plugged
plugging	*m.l.u.k.i.ng.*	plucking, plugging
plum	*m.l.u.m.*	blub, plum
plumber	*m.l.u.m.er.*	blubber, plumber
plume	*m.l.oo.m.*	bloom, plume
plump	*m.l.u.m.m.*	plump, *plum*
plunder	*m.l.u.t.t.er.*	blunder, blunter, plunder
plundered	*m.l.u.t.t.er.t.*	blundered, plundered
plundering	*m.l.u.t.t.er.i.ng.*	blundering, plundering
pod	*m.o.t.*	bot, pod, pot, *pond*
podded	*m.o.t.i.t.*	bonnet, podded, potted
podder	*m.o.t.er.*	podder, potter
pods	*m.o.t.s.*	pods, pots
poise	*m.oi.s.*	boys, buoys, poise
pole	*m.oh.l.*	bowl, mole, pole
poles	*m.oh.l.s.*	bowls, moles, poles
Pomp	*M.o.m.m.*	pomp, *bob, bomb, mob, mop, pop*
pond	*m.o.t.t.*	bond, pond, *pot*
pond	*m.o.t.t.*	pond, *bot, pod, pot*
pony	*m.oh.t.ee.*	bony, pony

poor	*m.aw.*	bore, moor, more, poor, pore
poorer	*m.aw.r.er.*	borer, poorer
pop	*m.o.m.*	bob, bomb, mob, mop, pop, *pomp*
popping	*m.o.m.i.ng.*	bobbing, bombing, mobbing, mopping, popping
pore	*m.aw.*	bore, moor, more, poor, pore
port	*m.aw.t.*	board, bored, born, bourne, bought, moored, pawned, poured, port
portal	*m.aw.t.a.l.*	mortal, portal
ported	*m.aw.t.i.t.*	boarded, ported
porter	*m.aw.t.er.*	boarder, border, mortar, mourner, pawner, porter
ports	*m.aw.t.s.*	boards, ports
pose	*m.oh.s.*	bows, pose
poses	*m.oh.s.i.s.*	poses, possess
possess	*m.oh.s.e.s.*	poses, possess
post	*m.oh.s.t.*	boast, most, post
posted	*m.oh.s.t.e.t.*	boasted, posted
posting	*m.oh.s.t.i.ng.*	boasting, posting
posts	*m.oh.s.t.s.*	boasts, posts
pot	*m.o.t.*	bot, pod, pot, *pond*

pots

pots	*m.o.t.s.*	pods, pots
potted	*m.o.t.e.t.*	bonnet, podded, potted
potter	*m.o.t.er.*	podder, potter
pounce	*m.ow.t.s.*	bounce, pounce, pouts, *bounds, pounds*
pound	*m.ow.t.t.*	bound, mound, mount, pound
pounded	*m.ow.t.t.e.t.*	mounted, pounded, *pouted*
pounding	*m.ow.t.t.i.ng.*	mounting, pounding
pounds	*m.ow.t.t.s.*	bounds, mounts, pounds, *bounce, pounce*
pounds	*m.ow.t.t.s.*	bounds, pounds, *bounce, pounce, pouts,*
poured	*m.aw.r.t.*	board, bored, born, bourne, bought, moored, pawned, poured, port
pouring	*m.aw.r.i.ng.*	boring, mooring, pouring
pouted	*m.ow.t.id*	pouted, *mounted, pounded*
pouts	*m.ow.t.s.*	bounce, pounce, pouts, *bounds, pounds*
power	*m.ow.er.*	bower, power
powers	*m.ow.er.s.*	bowers, powers
pox	*m.o.s.*	boss, box, moss, pox
poxed	*m.o.s.t.*	bossed, boxed, mossed, poxed

poxes	*m.o.s.i.s.*	bosses, boxes, mosses, poxes
practice	*m.r.a.k.t.i.s.*	practice, practise
practise	*m.r.a.k.t.i.s.*	practice, practise
praise	*m.r.ay.s.*	brace, braise, praise, prays
praised	*m.r.ay.s.t.*	brazed, praised
praises	*m.r.ay.s.i.s.*	braces, praises
praising	*m.r.ay.s.i.ng.*	braising, praising
prawn	*m.r.aw.t.*	broad, brawn, brought, prawn
pray	*m.r.ay.*	bray, pray, prey
prayed	*m.r.ay.t.*	brayed, prayed, preyed
prays	*m.r.ay.s.*	brace, braise, praise, prays
pressed	*m.r.e.s.t.*	breast, pressed
prey	*m.r.ay.*	bray, pray, prey
preyed	*m.r.ay.t.*	brayed, prayed, preyed
price	*m.r.ii.s.*	price, prize
prick	*m.r.i.k.*	brick, brig, prick, prig
pride	*m.r.ii.t.*	bride, bright, brine, pride
prig	*m.r.i.k.*	brick, brig, prick, prig
prim	*m.r.i.m.*	brim, prim
prize	*m.r.ii.s.*	price, prize
proud	*m.r.ow.t.*	browed, brown, proud

prow

prow	*m.r.ow.*	brow, prow
prows	*m.r.ow.s.*	brows, browse, prows
prude	*m.r.oo.t.*	brewed, brood, brute, prude, prune
prude	*m.r.oo.t.*	brood, brute, prude
prune	*m.r.oo.t.*	brewed, brood, brute, prude, prune
pub	*m.u.m.*	bum, mum, pub, pup, *bump, pump*
pudding	*m.uu.t.i.ng.*	pudding, putting
puddle	*m.u.t.l.*	muddle, puddle
puffed	*m.u.v.t.*	buffed, muffed, puffed
puffer	*m.u.v.er.*	buffer, puffer
puffin	*m.u.v.i.t.*	muffin, puffin
pug	*m.u.k.*	buck, bug, muck, mug, pug
pull	*m.uu.l.*	bull, pull
pulley	*m.uu.l.ee.*	bully, pulley
pulls	*m.uu.l.s.*	bulls, pulls
pump	*m.u.m.m.*	bump, pump, *bum, mum, pub, pup*
pumped	*m.u.m.m.t.*	bumped, pumped
pumps	*m.u.m.m.s.*	bumps, mumps, pumps, *bums, mums, pubs, pups*
pun	*m.u.t.*	bud, bun, but, butt, mud, pun, putt

pun	*m.u.t.*	bud, bun, but, butt, mud, pun, putt
punch	*m.u.t.j.*	bunch, munch, punch
punning	*m.u.t.i.ng.*	budding, bunting, butting, punning, punting, putting
puns	*m.u.t.s.*	buds, buns, butts, puns, putts
punting	*m.u.t.t.i.ng.*	budding, bunting, butting, punning, punting, putting
puolt	*m.oh.l.t.*	bold, bolt, mould, moult, poult
pup	*m.u.m.*	bum, mum, pub, pup, *bump, pump*
purser	*m.er.s.er.*	bursar, purser
pursued	*m.er.s.ew.t.*	pursued, pursuit
pursuit	*m.er.s.ew.t.*	pursued, pursuit
push	*m.uu.j.*	bush, push
pushed	*m.uu.j.t.*	bushed, pushed
pushes	*m.uu.j.iz*	bushes, pushes
pushing	*m.uu.j.i.ng.*	bushing, pushing
pushy	*m.uu.j.ee.*	bushy, pushy
puss	*m.uu.s.*	bus, puss
putt	*m.u.t.*	

putter

putter	m.u.t.er.	butter, mutter, putter
putting	m.uu.t.i.ng.	budding, bunting, butting, punning, punting, putting
putting	m.uu.t.i.ng.	pudding, putting
putts	m.u.t.s.	buds, buns, butts, puns, putts
putts	m.u.t.s.	butts, putts
putty	m.u.t.ee.	bunny, money, muddy, putty
puzzle	m.u.zzuu.l.	bustle, muscle, muzzle, puzzle
puzzled	m.u.s.l.t.	bustled, muscled, muzzled, puzzled
puzzles	m.u.zzuu.l.s.	bustles, muscles, muzzles, puzzles
quart	w.aw.t.	quart, *ward, warn, worn, wort*
quarter	w.aw.t.er.	quarter, *warder, water*
quartered	w.aw.t.er.t.	quartered, *watered*
quarters	w.aw.t.er.s.	quarters, *warders, waters*
quash	w.o.j.	quash, wash, watch
queen	w.ee.t.	queen, wean, weed
queer	w.ear.	queer, *weir*
quell	w.e.l.	quell, *well*
quest	w.e.s.t.	quest, *west*

question	*w.e.s.j.u.t.*	question, *questioned*
questioned	*w.e.s.j.u.t.*	questioned, *question*
quick	*w.i.k.*	quick, wick, wig
quicken	*w.i.k.uu.t.*	quicken, wicked, wicked
quids	*w.i.t.s.*	quince, quids, quins, quits, wince, winds, wins, wits
quill	*w.i.l.*	quill will
quills	*w.i.l.s.*	quills, wills
quince	*w.i.t.s.*	quince, quids, quins, quits, wince, winds, wins, wits
quins	*w.i.t.s.*	quince, quids, quins, quits, wince, winds, wins, wits
quipped	*w.i.m.t.*	quipped, whipped
quiried	*w.ia.r.i.t.*	quiried, *wearied*
quiry	*w.ia.r.ee.*	quiry, *weary*
quit	*w.i.t.*	quit, win, wind, wit
quite	*w.ii.t.*	quite, whine, white, wide, wind, wine
quits	*w.i.t.s.*	quince, quids, quins, quits, wince, winds, wins, wits
race	*r.ay.s.*	race, raise, rays
rack	*r.a.k.*	rack, rag

racking

racking	*r.a.k.i.ng.*	racking, ragging
racks	*r.a.k.s.*	racks, rags
rag	*r.a.k.*	rack, rag
rags	*r.a.k.s.*	racks, rags
raid	*r.ay.t.*	raid, rain, reign, rein, rate
raids	*r.ay.t.s.*	raids, rains, rates, reigns, reins
rain	*r.ay.t.*	raid, rain, reign, rein, rate
rains	*r.ay.t.s.*	raids, rains, rates, reigns, reins
raise	*r.ay.s.*	race, raise, rays
Ram	*R.a.m.*	ram, rap, wrap
rammed	*r.a.m.t.*	rammed, rapped, wrapped
rammer	*r.a.m.er.*	rammer, rapper, wrapper
rams	*r.a.m.s.*	rams, raps, wraps
ran	*r.a.t.*	ran, rat
rap	*r.a.m.*	ram, rap, wrap
rapped	*r.a.m.t.*	rammed, rapped, wrapped
rapper	*r.a.m.er.*	rammer, rapper, wrapper
raps	*r.a.m.s.*	rams, raps, wraps
rat	*r.a.t.*	ran, rat
rate	*r.ay.t.*	raid, rain, reign, rein, rate

rates	*r.ay.t.s.*	raids, rains, rates, reigns, reins
raw	*r.aw.*	raw, roar
rays	*r.ay.s.*	race, raise, rays
reasoned	*r.ee.s.o.t.t.*	reasoned, recent
rebel	*r.e.m.e.l.*	rebel, repel
rebelled	*r.i.m.e.l.*	rebelled, repelled
recent	*r.ee.s.u.t.t.*	reasoned, recent
red	*r.e.t.*	red, *rend, rent*
reek	*r.ee.k.*	reek, wreak
referred	*r.e.v.er.t.*	referred, revert
refers	*r.i.v.er.s.*	refers, reverse
reign	*r.ay.t.*	raid, rain, reign, rein, rate
reigns	*r.ay.t.s.*	raids, rains, rates, reigns, reins
reins	*r.ay.ns*	raids, rains, rates, reigns, reins
relief	*r.e.l.ee.v.*	relief, relieve
relieve	*r.e.l.ee.v.*	relief, relieve
remorse	*r.e.m.aw.s.*	remorse, *report*
rend	*r.e.t.t.*	rent, rend, *red*
rended	*r.e.t.t.i.t.*	rented, rended
rent	*r.e.t.t.*	rent, rend, *red*
rented	*r.e.t.t.e.t.*	rented, rended

repel

repel	*r.i.m.e.l.*	rebel, repel
repelled	*r.e.m.e.l.t.*	rebelled, repelled
report	*r.e.m.aw.t.*	report, *remorse*
reverse	*r.e.v.er.s.*	refers, reverse
revert	*r.e.v.er.t.*	referred, revert
rhyme	*r.ii.m.*	rhyme, rime, ripe, *crime*
rib	*r.i.m.*	rib, rim, rip
ribs	*r.i.m.s.*	ribs, rims, rips
rice	*r.ii.s.*	rice, rise
rich	*r.i.j.*	rich, ridge
rid	*r.i.t.*	rid, writ
ride	*r.ii.t.*	ride, right, rind, wright, write
rider	*r.ii.t.er.*	rider, writer
rides	*r.ii.t.s.*	rides, rights, writes
ridge	*r.i.j.*	rich, ridge
riding	*r.ii.t.i.ng.*	riding, writing
rids	*r.i.t.s.*	rids, rinse, writs
right	*r.ii.t.*	ride, right, rind, wright, write
rights	*r.ii.t.s.*	rides, rights, writes
rim	*r.i.m.*	rib, rim, rip
rime	*r.ii.m.*	rhyme, rime, ripe, *crime*
rims	*r.i.m.s.*	ribs, rims, rips

rind	*r.ii.t.t.*	ride, right, rind, wright, write
rinse	*r.i.t.s.*	rids, rinse, writs
rip	*r.i.m.*	rib, rim, rip
ripe	*r.ii.m.*	rhyme, rime, ripe, *crime*
rips	*r.i.m.s.*	ribs, rims, rips
rise	*r.ii.s.*	rice, rise
risen	*r.i.s.t.*	risen, wrist
road	*r.oh.t.*	road, rode, rote, rowed, wrote
roads	*r.oh.t.s.*	roads, robes
roam	*r.oh.m.*	roam, robe, ROME, rope
roar	*r.aw.*	raw, roar
robber	*r.o.m.er.*	robber, rotter
robbers	*r.o.m.er.s.*	robbers, rotters
robe	*r.oh.m.*	roam, robe, ROME, rope
robes	*r.oh.m.s.*	roads, robes
rod	*r.o.t.*	rod, RON, rot
rod	*r.o.t.*	rod, RON, rot
rode	*r.oh.t.*	road, rode, rote, rowed, wrote
rods	*r.o.t.s.*	rods, rots
role	*r.oh.l.*	role, *roll*
roll	*r.oh.l.*	roll, *role*

ROME

ROME	*R.OH.M.*	roam, robe, ROME, rope
root	*r.oo.t.*	root, route, rude
rope	*r.oh.m.*	roam, robe, ROME, rope
rose	*r.oh.s.*	rose, rows
rot	*r.o.t.*	rod, RON, rot
rote	*r.oh.t.*	road, rode, rote, rowed, wrote
rots	*r.o.t.s.*	rods, rots
rotted	*r.o.t.e.t.*	rotted, rotten
rotten	*r.o.t.e.t.*	rotted, rotten
rotter	*r.o.t.er.*	robber, rotter
rotters	*r.o.t.er.s.*	robbers, rotters
route	*r.oo.t.*	root, route, rude
rowed	*r.oh.t.*	road, rode, rote, rowed, wrote
rows	*r.oh.s.*	rose, rows
rub	*r.u.m.*	rub, rum
rudder	*r.u.t.er.*	rudder, runner
rude	*r.oo.t.*	root, route, rude
rum	*r.u.m.*	rub, rum
run	*r.u.t.*	run, rut
rung	*r.u.ng.*	rung, wrung
runner	*r.u.t.er.*	rudder, runner
runs	*r.u.t.s.*	runs, ruts

rut	*r.u.t.*	run, rut
ruts	*r.u.t.s.*	runs, ruts
sack	*s.a.k.*	sack, sag
sad	*s.a.t.*	sad, sat
sadder	*s.a.t.er.*	sadder, *sander*
safes	*s.ay.v.s.*	safes, saves
sag	*s.a.k.*	sack, sag
said	*s.e.t.*	said, set, *says, sex*
sail	*s.ay.l.*	sail, sale
sails	*s.ay.l.s.*	sails, sales
sale	*s.ay.l.*	sail, sale
sales	*s.ay.l.s.*	sails, sales
sat	*s.a.t.*	sad, sat
sauce	*s.aw.s.*	sauce, saws, source
sauces	*s.aw.s.e.s.*	sauces, sources
saves	*s.ay.v.s.*	safes, saves
saw	*s.aw.*	saw, sore
sawed	*s.aw.t.*	sawed, sort, sought, sword
saws	*s.aw.s.*	sauce, saws, source
says	*s.e.s.*	says, sex, *said, set*
scad	*s.k.a.t.*	scad, scan, scat, *scant*
scan	*s.k.a.t.*	scad, scan, scat, *scant*

scat

scat	*s.k.a.t.*	scad, scan, scat, *scant*
scene	*s.ee.t.*	cede, scene, seat, seed, seen
scenes	*s.ee.t.s.*	scenes, seats, seeds
scent	*s.e.t.t.*	cent, scent, send, sent
scents	*s.e.t.t.s.*	scents, sends, sense
screed	*s.k.r.ee.t.*	screed, screen
screen	*s.k.r.ee.t.*	screed, screen
sea	*s.ee.*	sea, see
seams	*s.ee.m.s.*	seams, seems, seeps
search	*s.er.j.*	search, surge
seashore	*s.ee.j.aw.*	seashore, *seesaw*
season	*s.ee.s.t.*	season, *ceased, seized, seasoned*
seasoned	*s.ee.s.u.t.t.*	seasoned, *ceased, season, seized*
seat	*s.ee.t.*	cede, scene, seat, seed, seen
seats	*s.ee.t.s.*	scenes, seats, seeds
seduce	*s.i.t.ew.s.*	secuce, *sinews*
see	*s.ee.*	sea, see
seed	*s.ee.t.*	cede, scene, seat, seed, seen
seeds	*s.ee.t.s.*	scenes, seats, seeds
seem	*s.ee.m.*	seem, seep

seemed	*s.ee.m.t.*	seemed, seeped
seems	*s.ee.m.s.*	seams, seems, seeps
seen	*s.ee.t.*	cede, scene, seat, seed, seen
seep	*s.ee.m.*	seem, seep
seeped	*s.ee.m.t.*	seemed, seeped
seeps	*s.ee.m.s.*	seams, seems, seeps
sees	*s.ee.s.*	cease, sees, seize
seesaw	*s.ee.s.aw.*	seesaw, *seashore*
seize	*s.ee.s.*	cease, sees, seize
seized	*s.ee.s.t.*	ceased, seized, *season, seasoned*
seized	*s.ee.s.t.*	season, *ceased, seized, seasoned*
seizing	*s.ee.s.i.ng.*	ceasing, seizing
self	*s.e.l.v.*	self, *shelf*
selfish	*s.e.l.v.i.j.*	selfish, *shell fish*
sell	*s.e.l.*	cell, sell
sellers	*s.e.l.er.s.*	cellars, sellers
sells	*s.e.l.s.*	cells, sells
send	*s.e.t.t.*	cent, scent, send, sent
sends	*s.e.t.t.s.*	scents, sends, sense
sense	*s.e.t.s.*	scents, sends, sense
sense	*s.e.t.s.*	sense, sets

sent

sent	*s.e.t.t.*	cent, scent, send, sent
serve	*s.er.v.*	serve, surf
server	*s.er.v.er.*	server, surfer
serves	*s.er.v.s.*	serves, surfs
service	*s.er.v.i.s.*	service, surface
set	*s.e.t.*	said, set, *says, sex*
sets	*s.e.t.s.*	sense, sets
sex	*s.e.s.*	says, sex, *said, set*
shade	*j.ay.t.*	chase, chased, chain, shade
sham	*j.a.m.*	chap, charm, jab, jam, sham, sharp
shame	*j.ay.m.*	jape, shame, shape
shamed	*j.ay.m.t.*	japed, shamed, shaped
shames	*j.ay.m.s.*	shames, japes, shapes
shape	*j.ay.m.*	jape, shame, shape
shaped	*j.ay.m.t.*	japed, shamed, shaped
shapes	*j.ay.m.s.*	japes, shames, shapes
share	*j.air.*	chair, share
shared	*j.air.t.*	chairs, shares, shared
shares	*j.air.s.*	chairs, shares, shared
shark	*j.a.k.*	jack, shark
sharp	*j.a.m.*	chap, charm, jab, jam, sham, sharp

shear	*j.ear.*	cheer, jeer, shear, sheer
shears	*j.ear.s.*	shears, jeered
shed	*j.e.t.*	jet, shed
sheds	*j.e.t.s.*	Jets, sheds
sheep	*j.ee.m.*	cheap, sheep
sheer	*j.ear.*	cheer, jeer, shear, sheer
sheet	*j.ee.t.*	cheese, cheat, sheet, jean, sheet
sheets	*j.ee.t.s.*	jeans, sheets, cheats
shen	*j.e.t.*	wed, wend, when, went, wet
sherry	*j.e.r.ee.*	cherry, sherry
ship	*j.i.m.*	chip, Jim, gym, ship
shipped	*j.i.m.t.*	chips, chipped, ships, shipped
ships	*j.i.m.s.*	chips, chipped, ships, shipped
shod	*j.o.t.*	John, jot, shod, shone, shot
shoes	*j.oo.s.*	choose, juice, shoes
shone	*j.o.t.*	John, jot, shod, shone, shot
shoot	*j.oo.t.*	June, shoot
shop	*j.o.m.*	chop, job, shop
shopping	*j.o.m.i.ng.*	chopping, shopping
shore	*j.aw.*	chore, jaw, shore

shored

shored	*j.aw.t.*	shored, shorn, short
shores	*j.aw.s.*	chores, jaws, shores
shorn	*j.aw.t.*	shored, shorn, short
short	*j.aw.t.*	shored, shorn, short
shot	*j.o.t.*	John, jot, shod, shone, shot
showed	*j.oh.t.*	showed, shown
shown	*j.oh.t.*	showed, shown
shows	*j.oh.s.*	chose, shows
side	*s.ii.t.*	side, sighed, sight, sign, site
sided	*s.ii.t.i.t.*	cited, sided, sighted, sited
sides	*s.ii.t.s.*	sides, sights, signs, sites
siding	*s.ii.t.i.ng.*	citing siding, sighning, sighting, siting
sighed	*s.ii.t.e.t.*	side, sighed, sight, sign, site
sight	*s.ii.t.*	side, sighed, sight, sign, site
sighted	*s.ii.t.i.t.*	cited, sided, sighted, sited
sighting	*s.ii.t.i.ng.*	citing siding, sighning, sighting, siting
sights	*s.ii.t.s.*	sides, sights, signs, sites
sign	*s.ii.t.*	side, sighed, sight, sign, site

signing	*s.ii.t.i.ng.*	citing siding, sighning, sighting, siting
signs	*s.ii.t.s.*	sides, sights, signs, sites
sin	*s.i.t.*	sin, sit
since	*s.i.t.s.*	since, *sinks*
sinews	*s.i.t.ew.s.*	sinews, *seduce*
sinks	*s.i.ng.k.s.*	sinks, *since*
sinks	*s.i.ng.k.s.*	sinks, *sings*
sinner	*s.i.t.er.*	sinner, sitter
sinners	*s.i.t.er.s.*	sinners, sitters
sit	*s.i.t.*	sin, sit
site	*s.ii.t.*	side, sighed, sight, sign, site
sited	*s.ii.t.i.t.*	cited, sided, sighted, sited
sites	*s.ii.t.s.*	sides, sights, signs, sites
siting	*s.i.t.i.ng.*	citing siding, sighning, sighting, siting
sitter	*s.i.t.er.*	sinner, sitter
sitters	*s.i.t.er.s.*	sinners, sitters
skid	*s.k.i.t.*	skid, skin, skit
skim	*s.k.i.m.*	skim, skip
skin	*s.k.i.t.*	skid, skin, skit
skip	*s.k.i.m.*	skim, skip
skit	*s.k.i.t.*	skid, skin, skit

slab

slab	s.l.a.m.	slab, slam, slap
slabbed	s.l.a.m.t.	slabbed, slammed, slapped
slabbing	s.l.a.m.i.ng.	slabbing, slamming, slapping
slack	s.l.a.k.	slack, slag
slag	s.l.a.k.	slack, slag
slam	s.l.a.m.	slab, slam, slap
slammed	s.l.a.m.t.	slabbed, slammed, slapped
slamming	s.l.a.m.i.ng.	slabbing, slamming, slapping
slap	s.l.a.m.	slab, slam, slap
slapped	s.l.a.m.t.	slabbed, slammed, slapped
slapping	s.l.a.m.i.ng.	slabbing, slamming, slapping
slid	s.l.i.t.	slid, slit
slide	s.l.ii.t.	slide, slight
slight	s.l.ii.t.	slide, slight
slim	s.l.i.m.	slim, slip
slimmed	s.l.i.m.t.	slimmed, slipped
slimmer	s.l.i.m.er.	slimmer, slipper
slimming	s.l.i.m.i.ng.	slimming, slipping
slims	s.l.i.m.s.	slims, slips
slip	s.l.i.m.	slim, slip

slipped	*s.l.i.m.t.*	slimmed, slipped
slipper	*s.l.i.m.er.*	slimmer, slipper
slipping	*s.l.i.m.i.ng.*	slimming, slipping
slips	*s.l.i.m.s.*	slims, slips
slit	*s.l.i.t.*	slid, slit
slob	*s.l.m.*	slob, slop
sloe	*s.l.oh.*	sloe, slow
slop	*s.l.o.m.*	slob, slop
sloped	*s.l.oh.m.t.*	sloped, *slowed*
slow	*s.l.oh.*	sloe, slow
slowed	*s.l.oh.t.*	slowed, *sloped*
smacked	*s.m.a.k.t.*	smacked, *sparked*
small	*s.m.aw.l.*	small, spall
smarts	*s.m.a.t.s.*	smarts, *spanned*
smear	*s.m.ear.*	smear, spear
smeared	*s.m.ear.t.*	smeared, speared
smears	*s.m.ear.s.*	smears, spears
smell	*s.m.e.l.*	smell, spell, *expel*
smelled	*s.m.e.l.s.*	smelt, smelled, spelled, spelt
smelling	*s.m.e.l.i.ng.*	smelling, spelling
smells	*s.m.e.l.s.*	smells, spells

smelt

smelt	*s.m.e.l.t.*	smelt, smelled, spelled, spelt
smelter	*s.m.e.l.t.er.*	smelter, spelter
smock	*s.m.o.k.*	smock, smog, *spot*
smog	*s.m.o.k.*	smog, smock, *spot*
smoke	*s.m.oh.k.*	smoke, spoke
smoked	*s.m.oh.k.t.*	smoked, *spoken*
snacks	*s.t.a.k.s.*	snacks, snags, stacks, stags
snags	*s.t.a.k.s.*	snacks, snags, stacks, stags
snail	*s.t.ay.l.*	snail, stale
snail	*s.t.ay.l.*	snail, stale, *dale, nail, tail, tale*
snails	*s.t.ay.l.s.*	snails, *dales, nails, tails, tales*
snake	*s.t.ay.k.*	snake, stake, steak
snaked	*s.t.ay.k.t.*	snaked, staked
snakes	*s.t.ay.k.s.*	snakes, stakes, steaks
snapped	*s.t.a.m.t.*	snapped, stabbed
sneer	*s.t.ear.*	sneer, steer
sneered	*s.t.ear.t.*	sneered, steered
snick	*s.t.i.k.*	snick, stick
snicks	*s.t.i.k.s.*	snicks, sticks
snob	*s.t.o.m.*	snob, stop

snore	*s.t.aw.*	snore, store
snore	*s.t.aw.*	snore, store
snout	*s.t.ow.t.*	snout, stout
snow	*s.t.oh.*	snow, stow
snowed	*s.t.oh.t.*	snowed, stoat, stone, stowed
snub	*s.t.u.m.*	snub, stub, stump
snuff	*s.t.u.v.*	snuff, stuff
snuffed	*s.t.u.v.t.*	snuffed, stuffed
snuffing	*s.t.u.v.i.ng.*	snuffing, stuffing
snuffs	*s.t.u.v.s.*	snuffs, stuffs
snug	*s.t.u.k.*	snug, stuck
sole	*s.oh.l.*	sole, soul
some	*s.u.m.*	some, sub, sum, sump, sup
son	*s.u.t.*	son, sun
sons	*s.u.t.s.*	sons, suds, suns
soon	*s.oo.t.*	soon, sued, suit
sooner	*s.oo.t.er.*	sooner, suiter
soot	*s.uu.t.*	soot, *soon*
sore	*s.aw.*	saw, sore
sort	*s.aw.t.*	sawed, sort, sought, sword

sought

sought	*s.aw.t.*	sawed, sort, sought, sword
soul	*s.oh.l.*	sole, soul
source	*s.aw.s.*	sauce, saws, source
sources	*s.aw.s.e.s.*	sauces, sources
space	*s.m.ay.s.*	space, *spade, spate*
spade	*s.m.ay.t.*	spade, spate, *space*
spall	*s.m.aw.l.*	small, spall
span	*s.m.a.t.*	span, spat
spanned	*s.m.a.t.t.*	spanned, *smarts*
spanner	*s.m.a.t.er.*	spanner, spatter
sparked	*s.m.a.k.t.*	sparked, *smacked*
spat	*s.m.a.t.*	span, spat
spate	*s.m.ay.t.*	spade, spate, *space*
spatter	*s.m.a.t.er.*	spanner, spatter
spawn	*s.m.aw.t.*	spawn, sport
speaks	*s.m.ee.k.s.*	speaks, *speeds*
spear	*s.m.ia.*	smear, spear
speared	*s.m.ia.t.*	smeared, speared
spears	*s.m.ia.s.*	smears, spears
sped	*s.m.e.t.*	sped, spend, spent
speeds	*s.m.ee.t.s.*	speeds, *speaks*
spell	*s.m.e.l.*	smell, spell, *expel*

spelled	*s.m.e.l.t.*	smelt, smelled, spelled, spelt
spelling	*s.m.e.l.i.ng.*	smelling, spelling
spells	*s.m.e.l.s.*	smells, spells
spelt	*s.m.e.l.t.*	smelt, smelled, spelled, spelt
spelter	*s.m.e.l.t.er.*	smelter, spelter
spend	*s.m.e.t.t.*	sped, spend, spent
spent	*s.m.e.t.t.*	sped, spend, spent
spilled	*s.m.i.l.t.*	spilled, spilt
spilt	*s.m.i.l.t.*	spilt, spilled
spin	*s.m.i.t.*	spin, spit
spine	*s.m.ii.t.*	spine, spite
spinning	*s.m.i.t.i.ng.*	spinning, spitting
spit	*s.m.i.t.*	spin, spit
spite	*s.m.ii.t.*	spine, spite
spitting	*s.m.i.t.i.ng.*	spinning, spitting
spoiled	*s.m.oi.l.t.*	spoiled, spoilt
spoilt	*s.m.oi.l.t.*	spoiled, spoilt
spoke	*s.m.oh.k.*	smoke, spoke
spoken	*s.m.oh.k.t.*	spoken, *smoked*
sport	*s.m.aw.t.*	spawn, sport
spot	*s.m.o.t.*	spot, *smock, smog*

squad

squad	*s.w.o.t.*	squad, squat
square	*s.w.air.*	square, swear
squaring	*s.w.air.r.i.ng.*	squaring,swearing
squat	*s.w.o.t.*	squad, squat
squaw	*s.w.aw.*	squaw, swore
stabbed	*s.t.a.m.t.*	snapped, stabbed
stabs	*s.t.a.m.s.*	stabs, stamps
stacks	*s.t.a.k.s.*	snacks, snags, stacks, stags
stags	*s.t.a.k.s.*	snacks, snags, stacks, stags
stain	*s.t.ay.t.*	stain, stayed, state
stains	*s.t.ay.t.s.*	stains, states
stair	*s.t.air.*	stair, stare
stake	*s.t.ay.k.*	snake, stake, steak
staked	*s.t.ay.k.t.*	snaked, staked
stakes	*s.t.ay.k.s.*	snakes, stakes, steaks
stale	*s.t.ay.l.*	snail, stale
stale	*s.t.ay.l.*	snail, stale, *dale, nail, tail, tale*
stammer	*s.t.a.m.er.*	stammer, *stamper*
stamper	*s.t.a.m.m.er.*	stamper, *stammer*
stamps	*s.t.a.m.m.s.*	stabs, stamps
stare	*s.t.air.*	stair, stare

state	*s.t.ay.t.*	stain, stayed, state
states	*s.t.ay.t.s.*	stains, states
stayed	*s.t.ay.t.*	stain, stayed, state
steak	*s.t.ay.k.*	snake, stake, steak
steaks	*s.t.ay.k.s.*	snakes, stakes, steaks
Steam	*S.t.ee.m.*	steam, steep
steep	*s.t.ee.m.*	steam, steep
steer	*s.t.ear.*	sneer, steer
steered	*s.t.ear.r.t.*	sneered, steered
stem	*s.t.e.m.*	stem, step
stemmed	*s.t.e.m.t.*	stemmed, stepped
stems	*s.t.e.m.s.*	stems, steps
step	*s.t.e.m.*	stem, step
stepped	*s.t.e.m.t.*	stemmed, stepped
steps	*s.t.e.m.s.*	stems, steps
stern	*s.t.er.t.*	stern, stirred
steward	*s.t.ew.er.t.*	steward, STUART
stick	*s.t.i.k.*	snick, stick
stile	*s.t.ii.l.*	stile, style
stirred	*s.t.er.t.*	stern, stirred
stoat	*s.t.oh.t.*	snowed, stoat, stone, stowed
stoats	*s.t.oh.t.s.*	stoats, stones

stone

stone	*s.t.oh.t.*	snowed, stoat, stone, stowed
stones	*s.t.oh.t.s.*	stoats, stones
stop	*s.t.o.m.*	snob, stop
store	*s.t.aw.*	snore, store
store	*s.t.aw.*	snore, store
stout	*s.t.ow.t.*	snout, stout
stow	*s.t.oh.*	snow, stow
stowed	*s.t.oh.t.*	snowed, stoat, stone, stowed
straight	*s.t.r.ay.t.*	straight, strain, strait, strayed
strain	*s.t.r.ay.t.*	straight, strain, strait, strayed
strained	*s.t.r.ay.t.t.*	strained, *strayed*
strait	*s.t.r.ay.t.*	straight, strain, strait, strayed
strayed	*s.t.r.ay.t.*	straight, strain, strait, strayed
strewed	*s.t.r.oo.t.*	strewed, strewn
strewn	*s.t.r.oo.t.*	strewed, strewn
strife	*s.t.r.ii.v.*	strife, strive
strim	*s.t.r.i.m.*	strim, strip
strimmed	*s.t.r.i.m.t.*	strimmed, stripped
strimmer	*s.t.r.i.m.er.*	strimmer, stripper
strims	*s.t.r.i.m.s.*	strims, strips

strip	*s.t.r.i.m.*	strim, strip
stripped	*s.t.r.i.m.t.*	strimmed, stripped
stripper	*s.t.r.i.m.er.*	strimmer, stripper
strips	*s.t.r.i.m.s.*	strims, strips
strive	*s.t.r.ii.v.*	strife, strive
struck	*s.t.r.u.k.*	struck, *shrug*
STUART	*S.T.EW.ER.T.*	steward, STUART
stub	*s.t.u.m.*	snub, stub, stump
stuck	*s.t.u.k.*	snug, stuck
stuff	*s.t.u.v.*	snuff, stuff
stuffed	*s.t.u.v.t.*	snuffed, stuffed
stuffing	*s.t.u.v.i.ng.*	snuffing, stuffing
stuffs	*s.t.u.v.s.*	snuffs, stuffs
stump	*s.t.u.m.m.*	snub, stub, stump
style	*s.t.ii.l.*	stile, style
sub	*s.u.m.*	some, sub, sum, sump, sup
submit	*s.u.m.m.i.t.*	submit, summit
subs	*s.u.m.s.*	subs, sums, sumps, sups
suds	*s.u.t.s.*	sons, suds, suns
sued	*s.oo.t.*	soon, sued, suit
suit	*s.oo.t.*	soon, sued, suit
suitor	*s.oo.t.er.*	sooner, suiter

sum

sum	*s.u.m.*	some, sub, sum, sump, sup
summed	*s.u.m.t.*	summed, supped
summer	*s.u.m.er.*	summer, supper
summing	*s.u.m.i.ng.*	summing, supping
summit	*s.u.m.i.t.*	submit, summit
sump	*s.u.m.m.*	some, sub, sum, sump, sup
sumps	*s.u.m.m.s.*	subs, sums, sumps, sups
sums	*s.u.m.s.*	subs, sums, sumps, sups
sun	*s.u.t.*	son, sun
sung	*s.u.ng.*	sung, *sunk*
sunk	*s.u.ng.k.*	sung, *sunk*
suns	*s.u.t.s.*	sons, suds, suns
sup	*s.u.m.*	some, sub, sum, sump, sup
supped	*s.u.m.t.*	summed, supped
supper	*s.u.m.er.*	summer, supper
supping	*s.u.m.i.ng.*	summing, supping
sups	*s.u.m.s.*	subs, sums, sumps, sups
surf	*s.er.v.*	serve, surf
surface	*s.er.v.i.s.*	service, surface
surfer	*s.er.v.er.*	server, surfer
surfs	*s.er.v.s.*	serves, surfs

surge	*s.er.k.*	search, surge
swab	*s.w.o.m.*	swab, swamp, swap
swabs	*s.w.o.m.s.*	swabs, swamps, swaps
swamp	*s.w.o.m.m.*	swab, swamp, swap
swamps	*s.w.o.m.m.s.*	swabs, swamps, swaps
swap	*s.w.o.m.*	swab, swamp, swap
swaps	*s.w.o.m.s.*	swabs, swamps, swaps
swear	*s.w.air.*	square, swear
swearing	*s.w.air.r.i.ng.*	squaring,swearing
swede	*s.w.ee.t.*	swede, sweet
sweet	*s.w.ee.t.*	swede, sweet
sword	*s.aw.t.*	sawed, sort, sought, sword
swore	*s.w.aw.*	squaw, swore
tab	*t.a.m.*	dab, dam, damn, damp, nab, nap, tab, tamp, tap
tabbed	*t.a.m.t.*	dabbed, dammed, damned,damped, knapped, nabbed, napped, tabbed, tamped, tapped
tabbing	*t.a.m.i.ng.*	dabbing, damming, nabbing, napping, tabbing, tamping, tapping, *napkin*
tabs	*t.a.m.s.*	dabs, dams, nabs, naps, tabs, tamps, taps

tack

tack	*t.a.k.*	knack, nag, tack, tag, *dank, tank*
tacked	*t.a.k.t.*	nagged, tacked, tact, *tanked*
tackle	*t.a.k.l.*	tackle, *dangle, tangle*
tad	*t.a.t.*	tad, tan, tat, *darn, dart, tarn, tarred, tart*
tag	*t.a.k.*	knack, nag, tack, tag, *dank, tank*
tags	*t.a.k.s.*	nags, tags, tax
tail	*t.ay.l.*	dale, nail, tail, tale, *snail, stale*
tails	*t.ay.l.s.*	dales, nails, tails, tales, *snails*
taken	*t.ay.k.t.*	bacon, taken
tale	*t.ay.l.*	dale, nail, tail, tale, *snail, stale*
tales	*t.ay.l.s.*	dales, nails, tails, tales, *snails*
tame	*t.ay.m.*	dame, name, nape, tame, tape
tamed	*t.ay.m.t.*	named, tamed, taped
tamer	*t.ay.m.er.*	neighbour, namer, tamer, taper
tames	*t.ay.m.s.*	dames, names, napes, tames, tapes
taming	*t.ay.m.i.ng.*	naming, taming, taping

tamped	*t.a.m.m.t.*	dabbed, dammed, damned,damped, knapped, nabbed, napped, tabbed, tamped, tapped
tamping	*t.a.m.m.i.ng.*	dabbing, damming, nabbing, napping, tabbing, tamping, tapping, *napkin*
tamps	*t.a.m.m.s.*	dabs, dams, nabs, naps, tabs, tamps, taps
tan	*t.a.t.*	tad, tan, tat, *darn, dart, tarn, tarred, tart*
tangle	*t.a.ng.l.*	dangle, tangle
tangled	*t.a.ng.k.l.t.*	dangled, tangled
tangling	*t.a.ng.k.l.i.ng.*	dangling, tangling
tanners	*t.a.t.er.s.*	natters, tanners, tatters
tap	*t.a.m.*	dab, dam, damn, damp, nab, nap, tab, tamp, tap
tape	*t.ay.m.*	dame, name, nape, tame, tape
taped	*t.ay.m.t.*	named, tamed, taped
taper	*t.ay.m.er.*	neighbour, namer, tamer, taper
tapes	*t.ay.m.s.*	dames, names, napes, tames, tapes
taping	*t.ay.m.i.ng.*	naming, taming, taping

tapped

tapped	*t.a.m.t.*	dabbed, dammed, damned,damped, knapped, nabbed, napped, tabbed, tamped, tapped
tapping	*t.a.m.i.ng.*	dabbing, damming, nabbing, napping, tabbing, tamping, tapping, *napkin*
taps	*t.a.m.s.*	dabs, dams, nabs, naps, tabs, tamps, taps
tarded	*t.a.t.i.t.*	darted, tarded, *daddy, dandy, natty, tatty*
target	*t.a.k.e.t.*	darken, target
tarn	*t.a.t.*	darn, dart, tarn, tarred, tart, *tan, tat*
tarred	*t.a.t.*	darn, dart, tarn, tarred, tart, *tan, tat*
tarts	*t.a.t.s.*	dance, darts, tarts,*stance*
tat	*t.a.t.*	tad, tan, tat, *darn, dart, tarn, tarred, tart*
tatters	*t.a.t.er.s.*	natters, tanners, tatters
tatty	*t.a.t.ee.*	daddy, dandy, natty, tatty, *darted, tarded, tanzy*
taught	*t.aw.t.*	dawn, gnawed, nought, torn, tort, toured, taught
taunting	*t.aw.t.t.i.ng.*	tauning,*dawning*
tax	*t.a.s.*	nags, tags, tax
TAY	*T.AY.*	day, neigh, TAY

tea	t.ee.	knee, tea
teacher	t.ee.j.er.	teacher, *t-shirt*
team	t.ee.m.	deem, deep, neap, team
teamed	t.ee.m.t.	deemed, teamed, teemed
teams	t.ee.m.s.	deems, deeps, teams, teems
tear	t.ear.	dear, deer, near, tear
tear	t.ear.	dear, near, tear
tearing	t.air.r.i.ng.	daring, tearing
tease	t.ee.s.	knees, niece, tease
teat	t.ee.t.	dean, deed, neat, need, teat, teen
teats	t.ee.t.s.	deans, deeds, needs, teats, teens
teemed	t.ee.m.t.	deemed, teamed, teemed
teems	t.ee.m.s.	deems, deeps, teams, teems
teen	t.ee.t.	dean, deed, neat, need, teat, teen
teens	t.ee.t.s.	deans, deeds, needs, teats, teens
tell	t.e.l.	dell, tell
ten	t.e.t.	dead, debt, den, net, ten, *dent,tent*

tended

tended	*t.e.t.t.e.t.*	tended, tented
tending	*t.e.t.t.i.ng.*	denting, tending, tenting
tense	*t.e.t.s.*	debts, dense, tense,*dents, tents*
tent	*t.e.t.t.*	dent, tent, *dead, debt, den, net, ten*
tented	*t.e.t.t.i.t.*	tended, tented
tenting	*t.e.t.t.i.ng.*	denting, tending, tenting
tents	*t.e.t.t.s.*	dents, tents, *debts, dense, tense*
terms	*t.er.m.s.*	terms, turps
terse	*t.er.s.*	nurse, terse
test	*t.e.s.t.*	nest, next, test, text
tether	*t.e.th.er.*	tether, never
text	*t.e.s.t.*	nest, next, test, text
than	*th.a.t.*	than, that
that	*th.a.t.*	than, that
their	*th.air.*	their, there
there	*th.air.*	their, there
thorns	*th.aw.t.s.*	thorns, thoughts
thoughts	*th.aw.t.s.*	thorns, thoughts
thread	*th.r.e.t.*	thread, threat
threat	*th.r.e.t.*	thread, threat

throat	*th.r.oh.t.*	throat, throne, thrown
throne	*th.r.oh.t.*	throat, throne, thrown
thrown	*th.r.oh.t.*	throat, throne, thrown
tick	*t.i.k.*	DICK, dig, nick, tick, tig
ticked	*t.i.k.t.*	nicked, ticked
ticker	*t.i.k.er.*	dicker, nicker, nigger, ticker
ticket	*t.i.k.i.t.*	dig it, nick it, ticket
ticking	*t.i.k.i.ng.*	digging, nicking, ticking
tickled	*t.i.k.l.t.*	niggled, tickled
ticks	*t.i.k.s.*	digs, nicks, ticks
tide	*t.ii.t.*	died, dine, dined, dyed, knight, night, nine, tide, tied, tight, tine
tides	*t.ii.t.s.*	dines, knights, nights, nines, tides, tights, tines
tidied	*t.ii.t.i.t.*	knighted, tidied
tidy	*t.ii.t.ee.*	tidy, tiny
tie	*t.ii.*	die, nigh, tie
tied	*t.ii.t.*	died, dine, dined, dyed, knight, night, nine, tide, tied, tight, tine
ties	*t.ii.s.*	dice, dyes, nice, ties
tig	*t.i.k.*	DICK, dig, nick, tick, tig

tight

tight	*t.ii.t.*	died, dine, dined, dyed, knight, night, nine, tide, tied, tight, tine
tightly	*t.ii.t.l.ee.*	nightly, tightly
tights	*t.ii.t.s.*	dines, knights, nights, nines, tides, tights, tines
tile	*t.ii.l.*	dial, tile
tiled	*t.ii.l.t.*	dialled, tiled
tiles	*t.ii.l.s.*	dials, tiles
till	*t.i.l.*	dill, nil, till
tilled	*t.i.l.t.*	tilled, tilt
tilt	*t.i.l.t.*	tilled, tilt
TIM	*T.I.M.*	dib, dim, dip, nib, nip, TIM, tip
timber	*t.i.m.m.er.*	dibber, dimmer, dipper, nipper, timber, tipper
timed	*t.ii.m.t.*	timed, typed
tin	*t.i.t.*	did, din, dint, knit, nit, tin, *didn't*
tine	*t.ii.t.*	died, dine, dined, dyed, knight, night, nine, tide, tied, tight, tine
tines	*t.ii.m.s.*	dines, knights, nights, nines, tides, tights, tines
tiny	*t.ii.t.ee.*	tidy, tiny
tip	*t.i.m.*	dib, dim, dip, nib, nip, TIM, tip

tipped	*t.i.m.t.*	dibbed, dimmed, dipped, nibbed, nipped, tipped,
tipper	*t.i.m.er.*	dibber, dimmer, dipper, nipper, timber, tipper
tipple	*t.i.m.uu.l.*	dimple, nimble, nipple, tipple
tipples	*t.i.m.uu.l.s.*	dimples, nipples, tipples
tips	*t.i.m.s.*	dips, dims, dips, nibs, nips, tips
tire	*t.ii.er.*	dire, tire, tyre
titch	*t.i.j.*	dish, ditch, niche, titch
titches	*t.i.j.i.s.*	dished, ditches, titches
to	*t.oo.*	do, to, too, two
toad	*t.oh.t.*	toad, tone, towed, *doe, dough, know, no, toe, tow*
toads	*t.oh.t.s.*	dotes, nodes, notes, toads, tones
toast	*t.oh.s.t.*	dosed, dozed, toast
toe	*t.oh.*	doe, dough, know, no, toe, tow, *toad, tone, towed*
toes	*t.oh.s.*	doze, knows, nose, toes
toffee	*t.o.v.ee.*	toffee, *coffee, copy*
tog	*t.o.k.*	dock, dog, knock, nog, tog

togs

togs	*t.o.k.s.*	docks, dogs, knocks, nogs, togs
toll	*t.o.l.*	doll, knoll, toll
TOM	*T.O.M.*	dob, knob, nob, TOM, top
tomb	*t.oo.m.*	doom, tomb
tombs	*t.oo.m.s.*	dooms, tombs
tome	*t.oh.m.*	dome, dope, gnome, tome
ton	*t.u.t.*	done, dud, none, nut, tonne, ton
tone	*t.oh.t.*	known, node, note, tone, tote
tone	*t.oh.t.*	toad, tone, towed, *doe, dough, know, no, toe, tow*
toner	*t.oh.t.er.*	donor, toner
tones	*t.oh.t.s.*	dotes, nodes, notes, toads, tones
tongue	*t.u.ng.*	dung, tongue, *dunk*
tonne	*t.u.t.*	done, dud, none, nut, tonne, ton
tonnes	*t.u.t.s.*	duds, nuns, nuts, tonnes, tons
tons	*t.u.t.s.*	duds, nuns, nuts, tonnes, tons
too	*t.oo.*	do, to, too, two

took	*t.uu.k.*	nook, took
top	*t.o.m.*	dob, knob, nob, TOM, top
topped	*t.o.m.t.*	dobbed, knobbed, topped
tore	*t.aw.*	door, gnaw, nor, tore, tour
torn	*t.aw.t.*	dawn, gnawed, nought, torn, tort, toured, taught
tort	*t.aw.t.*	dawn, gnawed, nought, torn, tort, toured, taught
toss	*t.o.s.*	doss, toss
tossed	*t.o.s.t.*	dossed, tossed
tossing	*t.o.s.i.ng.*	dossing, tossing
tot	*t.o.t.*	don, dot, knot, nod, non, not, tot
tote	*t.oh.t.*	known, node, note, tone, tote
tots	*t.o.t.s.*	dons, dots, knots, nods, tots
totted	*t.o.t.i.t.*	knotted, nodded, totted
touch	*t.u.j.*	dutch, touch
tough	*t.u.v.*	dove, tough
tour	*t.uu.er.*	door, gnaw, nor, tore, tour

toured

toured	t.*aw*.t.	dawn, gnawed, nought, torn, tort, toured, taught
tours	t.*aw*.s.	doors, gnaws, tours
toutes	t.*ow*.t.s.	doubts, downs, nouns,toutes, towns
tow	t.*oh*.	doe, dough, know, no, toe, tow, *toad, tone, towed*
towed	t.*oh*.t.	toad, tone, towed, *doe, dough, know, no, toe, tow*
towel	t.*ow*.u.l.	dowel, towel
tower	t.*ow*.er.	dower, tower
towing	t.*oh*.i.ng.	knowing, towing, *hoeing*
town	t.*ow*.t.	doubt, down, noun, nowt, town
towns	t.*ow*.t.s.	doubts, downs, nouns,toutes, towns
toys	t.*oi*.s.	noise, toys
track	t.*r*.*a*.k.	drag, track
tracked	t.*r*.*a*.k.t.	dragged, tracked
tracking	t.*r*.*a*.k.i.ng.	dragging, tracking
tracks	t.*r*.*a*.k.s.	drags, tracks
trade	t.*r*.*ay*.t.	drain, trade, train, trait
trader	t.*r*.*ay*.t.er.	drainer, trader,trainer, traitor

trades	*t.r.ay.t.s.*	drains, trades, trains, traits
trading	*t.r.ay.t.i.ng.*	draining, trading, training
traffic	*t.r.a.v.i.k.*	*terrific, travelled, raffled, ravelled, ravage*
train	*t.r.ay.t.*	drain, trade, train, trait
trained	*t.r.ay.t.t.*	drained, trained
trainer	*t.r.ay.t.er.*	drainer, trader,trainer, traitor
training	*t.r.ay.t.i.ng.*	draining, trading, training
trains	*t.r.ay.t.s.*	drains, trades, trains, traits
trait	*t.r.ay.t.*	drain, trade, train, trait
traitor	*t.r.ay.t.er.*	drainer, trader,trainer, traitor
traits	*t.r.ay.t.s.*	drains, trades, trains, traits
tram	*t.r.a.m.*	drab, dram, tram, tramp, trap
tramp	*t.r.a.m.m.*	drab, dram, tram, tramp, trap
tramps	*t.r.a.m.m.s.*	drams, trams, tramps, traps
trams	*t.r.a.m.s.*	drams, trams, tramps, traps
trap	*t.r.a.m.*	drab, dram, tram, tramp, trap

traps

traps	*t.r.a.m.s.*	drams, trams, tramps, traps
trawl	*t.r.aw.l.*	drawl, trawl
trawler	*t.r.aw.l.er.*	drawler, trawler
trawling	*t.r.aw.l.i.ng.*	drawling, trawling
tray	*t.r.ay.*	dray, tray
tread	*t.r.e.t.*	dread, tread
treads	*t.r.e.t.s.*	dreads, treads, trends
treble	*t.r.e.m.uu.l.*	treble, tremble
treks	*t.r.e.k.s.*	dregs, treks
tremble	*t.r.e.m.m.l.*	treble, tremble
trends	*t.r.e.t.t.s.*	dreads, treads, trends
tress	*t.r.e.s.*	dress, tress
tresses	*t.r.e.s.i.s.*	dresses, tresses
tribe	*t.r.ii.m.*	tribe, tripe
tried	*t.r.ii.t.*	dried, tried
trill	*t.r.i.l.*	drill, trill
trim	*t.r.i.m.*	drip, trim, trip
trimmed	*t.r.i.m.t.*	dripped, trimmed, tripped
trimming	*t.r.i.m.i.ng.*	dripping, trimming, tripping
trims	*t.r.i.m.s.*	drips, trims, trips
trip	*t.r.i.m.*	drip, trim, trip

tripe	*t.r.ii.m.*	tribe, tripe
tripped	*t.r.i.m.t.*	dripped, trimmed, tripped
tripping	*t.r.i.m.i.ng.*	dripping, trimming, tripping
trips	*t.r.i.m.s.*	drips, trims, trips
trod	*t.r.o.t.*	trod, trot
troll	*t.r.o.l.*	droll, troll
troop	*t.r.oo.m.*	droop, troop
trooped	*t.r.oo.m.t.*	drooped, trooped
troops	*t.r.oo.m.s.*	droops, troops, troupes
trot	*t.r.o.t.*	trod, trot
troupes	*t.r.oo.m.s.*	droops, troops, troupes
trout	*t.r.ow.t.*	drown trout
trove	*t.r.oh.v.*	drove, trove
truck	*t.r.u.k.*	drug, truck
trucks	*t.r.u.k.s.*	drugs, trucks
trudge	*t.r.u.j.*	drudge, trudge
truer	*t.r.oo.er.*	drew, true
trunk	*t.r.u.ng.k.*	drunk, trunk
trunks	*t.r.u.ng.k.s.*	drunks, trunks
trussed	*t.r.u.s.t.*	trussed, trust
trust	*t.r.u.s.t.*	trussed, trust
try	*t.r.ii.*	dry, try

trying

trying	*t.r.ii.y.i.ng.*	drying, trying
tub	*t.u.m.*	dumb, numb, tub, *dump*
tuck	*t.u.k.*	duck, dug, tuck, tug
tucked	*t.u.k.t.*	ducked, tucked
tucking	*t.u.k.i.ng.*	ducking, tucking, *dunking*
tug	*t.u.k.*	duck, dug, tuck, tug
tune	*t.ew.t.*	nude, newt, tune, *dune*
tuner	*t.ew.t.er.*	tuner, tutor
turd	*t.er.t.*	dirt, nerd, turd, turn
turds	*t.er.t.s.*	dirts, turds, turns
turkey	*t.er.k.ee.*	turkey, *dirty, turn key,*
turn	*t.er.t.*	dirt, nerd, turd, turn
turns	*t.er.t.s.*	dirts, turds, turns
turps	*t.er.m.s.*	terms, turps
tusk	*t.u.s.k.*	dusk, tusk
tutor	*t.ew.t.er.*	tuner, tutor
tweeds	*t.w.ee.t.s.*	tweeds, tweets
tweets	*t.w.ee.t.s.*	tweeds, tweets
twigs	*t.w.i.k.s.*	twigs,*twixt*
twin	*t.w.i.t.*	twin, twit
twit	*t.w.i.t.*	twin, twit
twixt	*t.w.i.s.t.*	twixt, *twigs*

two	*t.oo.*	do, to, too, two
tying	*t.ii.ee.i.ng.*	dying, tying
typed	*t.ii.m.t.*	timed, typed
tyre	*t.ii.er.*	dire, tire, tyre
urn	*er.t.*	earn, urn
vain	*v.ay.t.*	fade, fate, feign, fete, vain, vein, *faint*
van	*v.a.t.*	fad, fan, fat, van, vat
vary	*v.air.r.ee.*	fairy, vary
vast	*v.a.s.t.*	fast, vast
vaster	*v.a.s.t.er.*	faster, vaster
vastest	*v.a.s.t.e.s.t.*	fastest, vastest
vat	*v.a.t.*	fad, fan, fat, van, vat
vault	*v.aw.l.t.*	fault, vault
vaults	*v.aw.l.t.s.*	faults, vaults
veal	*v.ee.l.*	feel, veal
veer	*v.ee.er.*	fear, veer
veered	*v.ee.er.t.*	feared, veered
veering	*v.ee.r.i.ng.*	fearing, veering
veers	*v.ee.er.s.*	fears, veers
veil	*v.ay.l.*	fail, veil
vein	*v.ay.t.*	fade, fate, feign, fete, vain, vein, *faint*

vendor

vendor	*v.e.t.t.aw.*	vendor, *fender*
verb	*v.er.m.*	firm, verb
verse	*v.er.s.*	verse, *first, versed*
versed	*v.er.s.t.*	first, versed, *verse*
very	*v.e.r.ee.*	ferry, very
vet	*v.e.t.*	fed, fen, vet, *fend*
vetch	*v.e.j.*	fetch, vetch
vex	*v.e.s.*	fez, vex
vial	*v.ii.uu.l.*	file, vial, vile
vials	*v.ii.uu.l.s.*	files, vials
view	*v.ew.*	few, view
views	*v.ew.s.*	fuse, views
vigour	*v.i.k.er.*	figure, vigour
vile	*v.ii.l.*	file, vial, vile
vine	*v.ii.t.*	fight, find, fine, fined, vine, vined
vined	*v.ii.t.t.*	fight, find, fine, fined, vine, vined
vines	*v.ii.t.s.*	fights, fines, vines, *finds*
vision	*v.i.j.u.t.*	fission, vision, *fiction*
visions	*v.i.j.u.t.s.*	fission, vision, *fiction*
vital	*v.ii.t.uu.l.*	final, vital
vogue	*v.oh.k.*	folk, vogue, *foe*

volley	*v.o.l.ee.*	folly, volley
vote	*v.oh.t.*	phone, vote
voting	*v.oh.t.i.ng.*	phoning, voting
vowel	*v.ow.e.l.*	foul, fowl, vowel
vowels	*v.ow.l.s.*	fowls, vowels
wad	*w.o.t.*	wad, wand, want, watt, what
wade	*w.ay.t.*	wade, wain, wait, weighed, weight
waded	*w.ay.t.i.t.*	waded, waited
wader	*w.ay.t.er.*	wader, waiter
wading	*w.o.t.i.ng.*	wading, waiting
wads	*w.o.t.s.*	wads, wands, wants, watts
wafer	*w.ay.v.er.*	wafer, waiver, waver
wafers	*w.ay.v.er.s.*	wafers, waivers, wavers
waif	*w.ay.v.*	waif, waive, wave
waifs	*w.ay.v.s.*	waifs, waves
wain	*w.ay.t.*	wade, wain, wait, weighed, weight
waist	*w.ay.s.t.*	waist, waste, *ways*
wait	*w.ay.t.*	wade, wain, wait, weighed, weight
waited	*w.ay.t.e.t.*	waded, waited

waiter

waiter	*w.ay.t.er.*	wader, waiter
waiting	*w.ay.t.i.ng.*	wading, waiting
waive	*w.ay.v.*	waif, waive, wave
waiver	*w.ay.v.er.*	wafer, waiver, waver
waivers	*w.ay.v.er.s.*	wafers, waivers, wavers
wand	*w.o.t.t.*	wad, wand, want, watt, what
wands	*w.o.t.t.s.*	wads, wands, wants, watts
want	*w.o.t.t.*	wad, wand, want, watt, what
wants	*w.o.t.t.s.*	wads, wands, wants, watts
ward	*w.aw.t.*	ward, warn, worn, wort, *quart*
warder	*w.aw.t.er.*	warder, water, *quarter*
warders	*w.aw.t.er.s.*	warders, waters, *quarters*
ware	*w.air.*	ware, wear, where
warm	*w.aw.m.*	warm, warp
warmed	*w.aw.m.t.*	warmed, warped
warming	*w.aw.m.i.ng.*	Warming, warping
warn	*w.aw.t.*	ward, warn, worn, wort, *quart*
warp	*w.aw.m.*	warm, warp

warped	w.aw.m.t.	warmed, warped
warping	w.aw.m.i.ng.	Warming, warping
wash	w.o.j.	quash, wash, watch
washed	w.o.j.t.	washed, watched
washer	w.o.j.er.	washer, watcher
washing	w.o.j.i.ng.	washing, watching
waste	w.ay.s.t.	waist, waste, *ways*
watch	w.o.j.	quash, wash, watch
watched	w.o.j.t.	washed, watched
watcher	w.o.j.er.	washer, watcher
watching	w.o.j.i.ng.	washing, watching
water	w.aw.t.er.	warder, water, *quarter*
watered	w.aw.t.er.t.	watered, *quartered*
waters	w.aw.t.er.s.	warders, waters, *quarters*
watt	w.o.t.	wad, wand, want, watt, what
watts	w.o.t.s.	wads, wands, wants, watts
wave	w.ay.v.	waif, waive, wave
waver	w.ay.v.er.	wafer, waiver, waver
wavers	w.ay.v.er.s.	wafers, waivers, wavers
waves	w.ay.v.s.	waifs, waves
way	w.ay.	way, weigh

ways

ways	*w.ay.s.*	ways, *waist, waste*
weak	*w.ee.k.*	weak, week
weakly	*w.ee.k.l.ee.*	weakly, weekly
wean	*w.ee.t.*	queen, wean, weed
wear	*w.air.*	ware, wear, where
wearied	*w.ear.r.i.t.*	wearied, *quiried*
weary	*w.ear.r.ee.*	weary, *quiry*
weather	*w.e.th.er.*	weather, whether
wed	*w.e.t.*	wed, wend, when, went, wet
wed	*w.e.t.*	wed, wet, when
weed	*w.ee.t.*	queen, wean, weed
week	*w.ee.k.*	weak, week
weekly	*w.ee.k.l.ee.*	weakly, weekly
weigh	*w.ay.*	way, weigh
weighed	*w.ay.t.*	wade, wain, wait, weighed, weight
weight	*w.ay.t.*	wade, wain, wait, weighed, weight
weir	*w.ear.*	weir, *queer*
weld	*w.e.l.t.*	weld, welled, welt
well	*w.e.l.*	well, *quell*
welled	*w.e.l.t.*	weld, welled, welt
welt	*w.e.l.t.*	weld, welled, welt

wend	*w.e.t.t.*	wed, wend, when, went, wet
went	*w.e.t.t.*	wed, wend, when, went, wet
west	*w.e.s.t.*	west, *quest*
wet	*w.e.t.*	wed, wend, when, went, wet
wet	*w.e.t.*	wed, wet, when
what	*w.o.t.*	wad, wand, want, watt, what
wheeled	*w.ee.l.t.*	wheeled, wield
When	*W.e.t.*	wed, wet, when
where	*w.air.*	ware, wear, where
whether	*w.e.th.er.*	weather, whether
which	*w.i.j.*	which, wish, witch
whine	*w.ii.t.*	quite, whine, white, wide, wind, wine
whipped	*w.i.m.t.*	quipped, whipped
white	*w.ii.t.*	quite, whine, white, wide, wind, wine
whiten	*w.ii.t.uu.t.*	whiten, widen
whiter	*w.ii.t.er.*	whiter, wider
whites	*w.ii.t.s.*	whites, winds, wines
whole	*k.oh.l.*	coal, goal, hole, whole
wholly	*k.oh.l.ee.*	coley, holy, wholly
who's	*k.oo.s.*	who's, whose

whose

whose	*k.oo.s.*	who's, whose
wick	*w.i.k.*	quick, wick, wig
wicked	*w.i.k.e.t.*	quicken, wicked, wicked
wicket	*w.i.k.e.t.*	quicken, wicked, wicked
wicks	*w.i.k.s.*	wicks, wigs
wide	*w.ii.t.*	quite, whine, white, wide, wind, wine
widen	*w.ii.t.e.t.*	whiten, widen
wider	*w.ii.t.er.*	whiter, wider
widow	*w.i.t.oh.*	widow, window
widows	*w.i.t.oh.s.*	widows, windows
wield	*w.ee.l.t.*	wheeled, wield
wig	*w.i.k.*	quick, wick, wig
wigs	*w.i.k.s.*	wicks, wigs
will	*w.i.l.*	quill will
wills	*w.i.l.s.*	quills, wills
win	*w.i.t.*	quit, win, wind, wit
win	*w.i.t.*	quit, win, wind, wit
wince	*w.i.t.s.*	quince, quids, quins, quits, wince, winds, wins, wits
wind	*w.i.t.t.*	quit, win, wind, wit
wind	*w.i.t.t.*	quite, whine, white, wide, wind, wine
window	*w.i.t.t.oh.*	widow, window

windows	*w.i.t.t.oh.s.*	widows, windows
winds	*w.i.t.t.s.*	quince, quids, quins, quits, wince, winds, wins, wits
winds	*w.i.t.t.s.*	whites, winds, wines
windy	*w.i.t.t.ee.*	windy, WINNIE, witty
wine	*w.ii.t.*	quite, whine, white, wide, wind, wine
wines	*w.ii.t.s.*	whites, winds, wines
winner	*w.i.t.er.*	winner, winter
WINNIE	*W.I.T.EE.*	windy, WINNIE, witty
wins	*w.i.t.s.*	quince, quids, quins, quits, wince, winds, wins, wits
wins	*w.i.t.s.*	winds, wins, wits
winter	*w.i.t.t.er.*	winner, winter
wire	*w.ii.er.*	choir, wire
wires	*w.ii.er.s.*	choirs, wires
wish	*w.i.j.*	which, wish, witch
wit	*w.i.t.*	quit, win, wit
witch	*w.i.j.*	which, wish, witch
wits	*w.i.t.s.*	quince, quids, quins, quits, wince, winds, wins, wits
wits	*w.i.t.s.*	winds, wins, wits
witty	*w.i.t.ee.*	windy, WINNIE, witty

won

won	*w.u.t.*	one, won
wood	*w.uu.t.*	wood, would
worn	*w.aw.t.*	ward, warn, worn, wort, *quart*
wort	*w.aw.t.*	ward, warn, worn, wort, *quart*
would	*w.uu.t.*	wood, would
wrap	*r.a.m.*	ram, rap, wrap
wrapped	*r.a.m.t.*	rammed, rapped, wrapped
wrapper	*r.a.m.er.*	rammer, rapper, wrapper
wraps	*r.a.m.s.*	rams, raps, wraps
wreak	*r.ee.k.*	reek, wreak
wrench	*r.e.t.j.*	wrench, *wretch*
wrenches	*r.e.t.j.is*	wrenches, *wretches*
wretch	*r.e.j.*	wretch, *wrench*
wretches	*r.e.j.e.s.*	wretches, *wrenches*
wright	*r.ii.t.*	ride, right, rind, wright, write
wrist	*r.i.s.t.*	risen, wrist
writ	*r.i.t.*	rid, writ
write	*r.ii.t.*	ride, right, rind, wright, write
writer	*r.ii.t.er.*	rider, writer
writes	*r.ii.t.s.*	rides, rights, writes

writing	*r.ii.t.i.ng.*	riding, writing
writs	*w.i.t.s.*	rids, rinse, writs
wrote	*r.oh.t.*	road, rode, rote, rowed, wrote
wrung	*r.u.ng.*	rung, wrung
yard	*y.a.t.*	yard, yarn
yards	*y.a.t.s.*	yards, yarns
yarn	*y.a.t.*	yard, yarn
yarns	*y.a.t.s.*	yards, yarns
yore	*y.aw.*	yore, your
your	*y.aw.*	yore, your

Printed in Great Britain
by Amazon